Defining Violence
The Search for Understanding

Defining Violence
The Search for Understanding

David E Morrison

with

Brent MacGregor

Michael Svennevig

Julie Firmstone

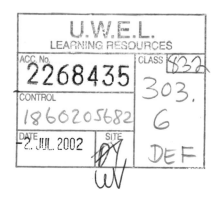
UNIVERSITY OF LUTON

Press

British Library Cataloguing in Publication Data
A catalogue record for this page is available from the British Library

ISBN: 1 86020 568 2

For Alison

Published by
University of Luton Press
Faculty of Humanities
University of Luton
75 Castle Street
Luton, Bedfordshire LU1 3AJ
United Kingdom
Telephone: +44 (0) 1582 743297; Fax: +44 (0) 1582 743298
e-mail: ulp@luton.ac.uk

Printed in Great Britain by Whitstable Litho Ltd,
Whitstable, Kent, United Kingdom

Contents

Preface

This volume presents the findings of research commissioned jointly by the BBC, the Broadcasting Standards Comm-ission, Channel Four Television, Channel 5 Broadcasting, the Independent Television Commission, the ITV Association, and British Sky Broadcasting. It followed an earlier pilot study conducted by Andrew Irving Associates.

Research conducted earlier in the 1990s by the University of Sheffield had provided objective 'counts' of the amount of violence across all television, and in many ways the study reported here takes off from where the Sheffield study ended, in that the current study took violent content to the audience and had viewers judge what they considered was serious violence and what was, although violent, not serious violence.

The task set the project team was a difficult one. What we wanted to know was the subjective meaning of violence. How, in other words, did people classify some acts as violent and other acts, although ostensibly violent, as not really violent? Did people, furthermore, have a common definition of violence, or were there many different definitions? The purpose of the research, therefore, was twofold. We, at the intellectual level, wanted to determine how violence was defined, and at the practical level to have information that would assist us in determining the perceived level of violence on television as opposed to the level as defined by some objective scoring that counted violence in say boxing or cartoons in similar fashion to violence appearing in the news or drama. The research was not concerned with taste – that is, whether viewers enjoyed or disliked a particular scene of screen violence – but rather with how violence was determined or defined.

There has been no lack of studies addressing the vexed question of the effects of screen violence on social behaviour. If anything this has been an obsessive concern of communications research, but perhaps surprisingly such work has gone on without addressing the meaning of violence, of what it is to consider one act involving damage to others as violent and other acts involving damage as not really violent. This study, therefore, represents a distinct departure in examining the question of screen violence.

The design of the study followed a strategy of deliberately focussing upon a wide variety of individuals who might stand differently to each other in their experience of, and attitudes towards, violence both in real life and on screen. The editing groups were recruited from tightly-defined segments of the population, including: policemen; young men and women drawn from cultural groups familiar with violence; women who had a heightened fear of, but no personal experience of, violence; women with small children; men with children. The intention of such sampling was to cast the recruitment net in such a way as to maximize the spectrum of understandings of violence, which would then allow the study the better to understand what was at work when someone defined an image as violent. By studying the meaning of violence from the variety of audience perspectives within the sample, the research would throw light on the key question of whether or not there is a centrally agreed definition of violence, or whether there exist different definitions. If the latter was the case, then depending on the number and range of definitions, what constituted violence would remain relatively elusive in terms of establishing the amount of screen violence.

Finally, it it should be noted that the task of addressing the complex issues involved in understanding how viewers define violence involved close analysis and intricate working by the Leeds researchers. On behalf of the organisations which commissioned the research, I edited and simplified the report originally submitted by Dr Morrison and his colleagues to make it more readily accessible to the non-specialist reader. No doubt some of their arguments have been over-simplified, but I hope that nothing has been distorted.

Robert Towler
Independent Television Commission

1

Introduction

ike the pilot research conducted for the television industry
consortium by Andrew Irving Associates, the research
reported here tried to answer the question, 'How do viewers
define violence?'*

In the course of answering this question several issues were addressed.
We looked at the acceptability of violence; whether violence is
enjoyed; the justification of screen violence, and the effect that the
type of programme had on the definition and acceptability of
violence. At all times the research focused on the central problem of
what is defined as violence, and how this definition varies.
Throughout, we tried to understand the factors at play when
someone categorises an act as violent. As part of the exercise we tried
to discover whether there is a single definition of violence.

Methods

We used 'video editing groups', a technique developed by the
Institute of Communications Studies of the University of Leeds to
explore how viewers perceive and understand screen violence.
Straightforward video images, or 'video grabs' as employed by
Andrew Irving, are often shown in the course of conventional focus
groups, but the comments made by respondents are not sufficiently
focused on the structure and content of what is shown.

---

* *Copies of the Report of research conducted by Andrew Irving Assocaites are
available from the Information Office, ITC, 33 Foley Street, London
W1P 7LB.*

'Video editing', on the other hand, allows respondents to act as their own editors. By making, or suggesting, cuts or other alterations, respondents helped us clarify exactly what they meant by violence. In making an edit respondents were forced to confront the reason for their decision, and the act of editing helped them articulate meanings they might otherwise have found impossible to express. Editing can be used to take respondents through their own thought processes in a way not open to verbal probing by itself.

We used a digital editing machine to see what difference it made if we – rather than the respondents – altered material. We did this to assess how far outside factors (like sound levels or background laughter) influence the perception of violence. It is worth mentioning, however, that only on very few occasions did we resort to this procedure, and in reporting the findings we shall make clear when the editing, or introduction of variables, was done by the researchers.

The sample

The sample consisted of 12 groups of eight respondents, and was broadly representative of age, gender, and social grade. The sample was drawn from Scotland, Northern England, Midlands, London and the South West. In addition to standard demographic sampling, respondents were recruited to provide as wide a range of responses as possible, by including individuals with characteristics or experiences that might give added insight into how violence is defined. In this respect our sample was strikingly different from Andrew Irving's.

Each of our groups was made up of individuals who might be expected to regard screen violence in a particular way. The representativeness of the sample derived from the spread produced by all 12 groups. The individual groups were decidedly unrepresentative. For example, young men familiar with violence were recruited. So were young women familiar with violence. Policemen, familiar with the effects of violence, formed another group. Combat veterans of the Second World War were represented. Women with a fear of crime were recruited, and so were parents with young children. Cable and satellite viewers who subscribed to film channels were also represented in the sample. The field work was undertaken in November and December 1997 (see Appendix 1 for sample).

Visual material used

A wide range of visual material was used during the editing groups. It included three Hollywood films, two British realist films, and two British made-for-television dramas. Actuality material was also shown, including news footage from ITN, the BBC, Croatian television (HRT) and Sky News. Untransmitted news agency pictures were shown, and documentary and current affairs material was included. Violence in comedy, cartoons and children's programmes also formed part of the package of material shown (see Appendix 2 for full description of the material used).

Organisation of the report

There were two obvious ways of organising this report: first, by reporting all the responses to each piece of material, so that each clip shown to the respondents is discussed in some kind of sequence; second, by taking the responses of each group in turn. We have opted for the latter, but in doing so we will also make cross references to other groups where we consider comparative comment will illuminate a point. No attempt will be made to exhaust all points that were made. Our task is to discover what people mean when they say something is violent. The report will finish by attempting to pull the material together in schematic form to provide an overview of the factors which influence a definition of violence.

The space given to each successive group becomes less as the report progresses, because later groups often repeated points made by earlier groups. With later groups we concentrated on the special features for which the group was recruited, to find out whether these inclined them to define violence differently from the other groups.

Terminology

The present research shows that it is not particular acts which make a programme seem violent, but the context in which they occur. Using a sample broadly representative of the UK population,

Andrew Irving Associates found that reactions to screen violence divided into five main types: Enthusiasts; Unqualified Acceptors; Qualified Acceptors; Qualfied Rejecters; and Rejecters. As far as screen output was concerned, the Andrew Irving respondents categorised violence under five headings: 'Fantasy/harmless'; 'Historical/Educational'; 'Everyday family drama'; 'Real life'; and 'Adult drama'.

Andrew Irving also showed that viewers distinguish between 'violence with a little v' (violence in name only, which doesn't matter) and 'violence with a big V' (serious violence, which does).

We have adopted this usage, and added the term 'massive V' for exceptionally strong violence. Even a particularly bloody scene remains 'violent with a little v' if it lacks the context to make it fully violent. It is not defined as truly violent, but more as an act of violent display. Much violence seen on television is of this order, and not seriously disturbing to the sensibilities of viewers.

Three types of violence

We have split screen violence into three types: playful violence, depicted violence, and authentic violence.

Playful violence is clearly acted violence, and is seen as unreal. The violence looks staged, and has little significance beyond its entertainment value. It is invariably seen as violence with a little v. A lot of violent action may be involved, but it is not graphic and does not assault the sensibilities.

Depicted violence is violence that is characterised by 'realism'. It attempts to depict violence as it would appear in real life. It often includes close-up shots of injury, and is very graphic. This can indeed assault the sensibilities, and is invariably defined as violence with a big V.

Authentic violence is violence set in a world that the viewer can recognise. A classic case would be domestic violence. Violence in a pub or shopping precinct might be other examples. It is closer to the life of the viewer than other forms of violence. It might be seen as violence with a little v, depending on how the scene is played, although it does have the potential to be big V, and even massive V.

In other words it has the possibility of assaulting the sensibilities very strongly indeed.

These are all fictional categories of violence. 'Real life' screen violence – news footage, documentary footage and so on - we have called 'actuality' material.

The respondents themselves did not distinguish between playful, depicted and authentic violence. But, using their estimate of how violent a programme was, we have put each programme into one of the three categories. For example, the domestic violence in *Ladybird, Ladybird* is labelled authentic violence (massive V); the violence in *Deep Cover* is labelled depicted violence (big V); and the violence in *Thief Takers* is labelled playful violence (little v).

It is not simple to make these distictions absolute, since so much depends on how a scene is shot. For instance, authentic violence may be overlaid by depicted violence – that is, the violence in an authentic setting may be given a realistic treatment, looking as it would have looked had the viewer witnessed such a scene in real life.

The inter-relationship of our three categories of violence can be summed up as follows:

	PLAYFUL	DEPICTED	AUTHENTIC
WEAK	Always	Never	Sometimes
STRONG	Never	Always	Sometimes
MASSIVE	Never	Never	Sometimes

These categories have been very useful in distinguishing between different kinds of violent scenes, but they have not answered the central question: what makes something violent?

Definers of violence

Discussion with the participants revealed that two factors determine whether a scene is perceived as violent. The first was the *nature and quality* of the violence portrayed, and the second was the *way in which* it was portrayed.

The two factors are moral and artistic respectively, and together they determine the definition of violence. The elements which make up factor one we have called the *primary definers* of violence, and those which contribute to factor two we have called the *secondary definers* of violence.

The primary definers come into play first. If a scene is violent in terms of the primary definers, then the secondary definers come into play in grading the level of violence perceived.

Primary definers

Primary definers of violence are drawn from real life, and what is deemed violent on screen is the same as what is deemed violent in real life. An act is defined as violent in real life if it breaks a recognised and mutually agreed code of conduct. Take the example of a fight in a pub. It would undoubtedly be considered a violent act for one person to punch or slap another in a pub, but nevertheless, for certain individuals, under certain circumstances, it might be considered appropriate behaviour, and not to be violent in any serious sense. On the other hand there are no circumstances under which one person 'glassing' another would fall within a recognised and mutually agreed code of conduct, and it would unambigiously be judged a violent act. This is true in real life, and it is true on screen. So what constitutes violence is an act which breaks a recognised code of behaviour.

An act may be seen as seriously violent in one situation, but trivial in another. But, as we have seen from the example of 'glassing', some acts are universally proscribed. There seem to be some general principles which underlie all proscriptions of violence, although the type of act proscribed may vary between different cultures. The most prevalent general rule seems to be that behaviour which is judged to be appropriate, fair and justified – even when overtly violent – is not usually seen to be seriously or 'really' violent.

Participants frequently used the principle of fairness to decide whether an act was violent or not. It was considered by all our respondents that to act violently you had to break a code of conduct governing physical exchange, and the code was always based on fairness or justice. We shall see repeatedly that in judging a particular scene as violent or not, respondents referred to power relationships: something was violent if the assailant was stronger than the victim; if the victim was disadvantaged in some way; or if the victim could not respond on equal terms to the assailant.

An act was also considered violent if it was unjust in the sense that the violence inflicted was out of all proportion to what was merited – where the extent of the injury was not warranted, or where the injury continued longer than was deserved.

Secondary definers

Once respondents had reached a judgement that the violence shown was unfair, and thus the 'primary definers' were operating, they followed this by grading the level of violence by applying the secondary definers of violence. It is the secondary definers of violence – how the violence is portrayed – that establish the degree of violence perceived by the viewer.

The secondary definers categorise a scene as violent if it looks 'real' – as the viewer imagines it would if witnessed in real life. Close-up shots of an injury, and splattering blood, both make violence look 'real'. So does the manner in which an injury is delivered, and how it is portrayed. Each of these elements helps to produce a greater sense of violence once the primary definers have established the scene to be violent in the first place.

For example, the domestic violence seen in *Brookside* and the domestic violence seen in *Ladybird, Ladybird* both constituted primary definitions of violence (a man hitting a woman was held to be wrong, and in both cases the disparities in strength made the behaviour unfair). But the violence in *Ladybird, Ladybird* was considered massively more violent than that seen in *Brookside* because the secondary definers of violence were present more strongly: the blows were repeated, and were delivered more heavily, the wife suffered severe injury, and the whole delivery of the violence was accompanied by threatening language.

These findings show that there is considerable agreement between people about what *is* violent, and also about the *level* of violence in a scene. But while agreement over what *is* violent is based on real life, the *level* of violence is judged not by real life, but by what has been learned from watching violence on the screen.

The respondents measured levels of violence by its 'realism'. But most participants had never witnessed in real life the sort of violence shown to them. They therefore had no way of knowing if the portrayals were 'realistic' or not. They seemed to be deciding whether screen violence was 'realistic' by comparing it with other screen portrayals.

In the course of the report we shall refer at various points to 'the new rules of injury'. These are the changing conventions employed by film-makers to give more and more 'realism' to violent injury: to attempt to show injuries as they would supposedly look in real life, with clinical precision. To achieve the impression of reality, the media version of violence is made more 'real' than the real thing. People may die slowly, for example, but they do not die in slow motion, as they often do on screen.

We have said that 'realism' is a key secondary definer of violence, determining how violent a sequence is seen to be. It would seem, however, that 'realism' is recognised only by reference to conventions established by previous directors, and now familiar to the audience. For example, if Tarrantino creates a graphic and exaggerated image of a bullet wound, other executions that fall short of Tarrantino's will not be seen as realistic accounts of what violence looks like, and therefore will not be seen as particularly violent. Indeed, mention was made in the groups to past programmes which were considered violent at the time, but, when shown now, appear tame because the violence is old-fashioned.

Generalisation of the findings

One cannot use the findings of qualitative research to generalise about the population as a whole. Focus groups can suggest the range of opinions held by the population at large, but they cannot establish the distribution of those opinions. However, the results of this research may well give some indication of the views of the wider population. We have already indicated the breadth of our sample, but even with this wide cross section of opinion we failed to find serious differences between the groups as to what constitutes violence. If basic differences did exist, some indication of them would almost certainly have emerged, given the disparate nature of our sample.

In fact, basic differences about defining violence did not exist among our participants, and we feel confident that we can provide a general definition of what constitutes screen violence. From the findings, this working definition of violence emerged:

> *Screen violence is any act that is seen or unequivocally signalled which would be considered an act of violence in real life, because the violence was considered unjustified either in the degree or nature of the force used, or that the injured party was undeserving of the violence. The degree of violence is defined by how realistic the violence is considered to be, and made even stronger if the violence inflicted is considered unfair.*

2

Hard Men and a Hard Case – or Chin up, she asked for it

We begin with the hard men. These were single, living in London, aged between 18 and 24. One of the recruitment criteria for 'hardness' was a familiarity with violence, defined as having been regularly close to violence. We did not ask if they themselves were instigators of violence. Instead, we sought simply to recruit people who lived in a world of which violence was a salient feature.

Experience of violence

Conversation with this group revealed a world in which fights were expected. Although it would be wrong to say they had a casual attitude to real life violence, it was quite clear that to witness violence did not shock them, as it might most people. Even so – and this is relevant to screen violence – real life violence was not continuous, and an act was judged violent depending on the nature of the damage inflicted, perceived culpability and so on. Most fights appeared to involve drink. When one of the respondents was asked, 'Have you ever been caught up in violence?', he replied:

Not apart from sometimes in clubs when someone gets drunk and picks a fight.

Questioned as to whether they had ever 'seen any really nasty stuff', most agreed that they had. When pressed to define nasty, one person replied:

When someone gets hit with a glass.

Someone else added:

It's mostly when someone been drinking too much.

Other comments followed:

I saw someone's face slashed with a Stanley knife about a year ago.

I saw someone killed a few weeks ago — he got stabbed.

The person stabbed to death turned out to have been a close friend of the respondent. Glassing, stabbing, slashing with a Stanley knife are, as we shall see, good indicators of violence in real life that can be used to define violence as portrayed on the screen.

[Prompt] What about fist fights, would you classify them as very violent?

It depends — sometimes it's all over very quickly, and sometimes you see people really get hurt.

A fist fight, the most common form of pub brawl, is real enough, but does not necessarily qualify as violent. The degree of violence depends on the form the fight takes, and, as the above young man noted, whether a fist fight is violent or not depends on its duration and on the degree of harm inflicted.

A 'realistic' screen fist fight, that was over very quickly, would not readily be classified as violent, whereas it might be if the fight continued for a long time. Prolonging the fight makes it unrealistic compared with a fight in real life, but makes it more 'realistic' in cinematic terms. Repeated blows or prolonged inflicting of pain transforms small v violence into big V by becoming savage.

So often a film-maker's attempts to be 'realistic', such as in *Full Metal Jacket*, or *Platoon*, become highly unrealistic, bearing no resemblnce to what someone who was actually present would have seen.

In the real world, a violent event is often over in seconds or less, and a fist fight might consist of one blow, as all the respondents with first hand experience of violence testified. Screen violence is often exaggerated, stretched — indeed often shot in slow motion. Mundane events, such as crossing a room or answering a telephone, are shortened on screen. Abnormal events, such as violent eruptions, are often prolonged for dramatic effect. The final scene in *Bonnie and Clyde*, and the *Thief Takers* material used in this research, are both examples of the use of this device. Earlier research using the editing method (Morrison

& MacGregor, in Millwood Hargrave, *Violence in Factual Television*, BSC, 1993) drew attention to the dramatic effect of stylised slow motion.

These techniques cannot be called 'realistic' in any truthful sense of the term, but they are perceived as adding realism to a scene, and thereby increasing its violence.

Because these young men were no strangers to violence they were asked whether they considered that repeatedly watching violence on television dulled their sensitivity to real life violence.

> *[Prompt] One of the arguments is that if you watch a lot of violence on television, then when you see real life violence it doesn't bother you so much. Do you think that's true?*
>
> *It's totally different when you see it out on the streets.*

We asked what was the difference:

> *There's not so much noise for a start.*
>
> *People who get hit actually fall over sometimes and don't get up. People can get shot 20 times on some films and then get up.*

Real life violence was seen as different, and more disturbing than screen violence. The young man whose friend had been knifed to death, was asked whether the stabbing was 'worse than anything you've seen on television'?

> *Yes, it was a lot worse. It was like a normal fight, but then somebody pulled out a knife.*

He said he was upset by the scene, and commented:

> *It's a lot different to watching it on TV. TV's nothing like real life.*

The question of screen violence desensitising viewers to real life violence will be returned to with other groups.

Rules of injury & reality

Real life violence is disturbing because it is real. It is not part of some other world, but the world of immediate experience, placing the individual in direct relationship to the act. The individual witnessing real life violence is present at the event and part of it. For most people the everyday world assumes the absence of violence, so when violence does occur the mundane reality is broken, and as with any break in a familiar pattern the response is one of shock.

Even with these 'hard' young men, who were accustomed to violence, the violence that they knew did not occur in a random and unpredictable fashion, but was located at sites where violence could be expected, like places of entertainment where alcohol was served. The group was asked if they went into a pub that was renowned for fights and got beaten up, 'Would it be their own fault'? Although not quite agreeing that it would be their own fault, there was some agreement: 'You've got to expect it if you go in there', suggesting a degree of predictability.

We shall see the importance of rules in defining violence once we begin to examine actual clips of violence, but for the moment it is worth noting not only that human conventions govern what is seen as violent, but that screen genres also have rules, and if those rules are understood, it is less likely that acts of violence will be seen as especially violent. Once learnt by the viewer, the rules protect the individual from being shocked by violence, indeed they enable the viewer to see screen violence as no more than 'little v', until, that is, the violence breaks the existing rules. Tarrantino's films have meant that a new set of rules governing the portrayal of violence have had to be learnt. We can hazard a guess that if older people find modern screen violence unpleasant, they have not kept abreast of the changing rules. If they haven't seen much modern film, a chance exposure to new rules governing violence breaks the bounds of the expected and the understood.

Out of order & rules

These young men, even though they themselves engage in fights, occupy a world in which rules regulate violent conduct. They were shocked, and defined an act as violent, when that violence went beyond what might be expected or even deserved. A fist fight was not necessarily violent, but slashing with a Stanley knife was, because it broke the accepted rules of aggressive physical exchange. Such behaviour did shock, and did so because – to use a phrase popular with them – it was 'out of order'. Indeed, the very phrase, 'out of order', indicates the acceptance of rules, even in the area of violence, which by its nature is not easily amenable to rules. It was quite clear that these 'hard' young men existed in a world where the power of persuasive reason was not given much respect, and whose inhabitants tended to value force and physical prowess. As far as we could tell, they were not lawless, but in their culture the ability to 'handle oneself' was necessary. They talked easily of 'chinning' someone who was 'out of order'. And their acceptance of violence influenced their definition of screen violence, especially in cases where the screen violence was similar to situations they could imagine in their own lives.

Director-driven definitions of violence

Even so, it must be remembered that when asked to compare real life violence and screen violence a distinction was drawn. For example, they said that in real life fighting was not accompanied by the same level of noise as on screen. And yet, despite this distinction, and despite saying that television violence is 'nothing like real life', screen violence was judged by its faithfulness to 'real life violence' (in fact, imagined real life violence, since much screen violence is of a type that even these 'hard' young men would not have experienced).

This apparent anomaly explains how definitions of violence arise. Much of what is accepted as 'realistically' violent is merely the latest cinematic fashion in violence. It is the 'rules of injury' that determine what the viewer accepts as violence, and the 'rules of injury' are constantly changing.

We shall see later how a news item showing the nearly severed head of a woman's body, hanging almost by a thread of tissue after she been hit by a mortar shell, was not seen by many viewers as 'real'. Real it was, but to the viewers the picture did not look like a screen war injury. It had a naturalness which, if recreated fictionally, would have looked false, because it could not dramatically have made a statement about the drama of death: she looked more like a mannequin than a person. In another scene from Bosnia a headless body is lifted into a truck by his jacket, and many viewers did not realise that the body had no head. They presumed instead that his jacket had ridden up over his head in the process of being lifted.

We are not saying that fictional portrayals of violence are not a reflection of what occurs in real life – that injuries would not look as they are made to look. But we are saying that injuries do not always look as they appear on screen. Of all the permutations of injury that are possible in real life, the screen has selected only the more photogenic examples, and elevated them into the definition of what violence looks like. Screen violence has not become more realistic in the sense of capturing the real, but film 'realism' has been established so strongly that it has become the definition of violence.

Thief Takers: playful violence

Let us now look at how these 'hard' young men viewed images of violence, and start with a discussion of realism. We began the session, as we did all the sessions, by showing *Thief Takers*. In this clip, Russian gangsters break into a meeting of British gangsters in a restaurant, and attempt to muscle in on their business. The police are tracking the Russian gangsters and burst in to arrest them. There is much gun play, blood, and flying backwards over tables in slow motion as individuals are hit by automatic pistol fire.

Following the clip we put the question: 'Was that violent?'

> *So so.*
>
> *I wouldn't say it was violence – it was television violence wasn't it. It was no more than what you see at least once a day on television.*
>
> *I thought it was a bit ridiculous – the fact that they were spraying the machine gun right, left and centre and none of the police seem to get hit.*
>
> *You see that sort of thing every day on the telly.*

No one wanted to edit this clip. It was seen as not violent, 'so so', or violent with a little v, because it was 'ridiculous', or, expressed another way, because it was entertainment or narrative violence, with no intention other than provide excitement – it gave 'pace' to the drama.

Even though none of these 'hard' men had experienced or witnessed such violence in real life, it took little effort or imagination to recognise that the shootings were not meant as a representation of anything occurring in real life – the violence was not 'real', nor was the violence a believable reconstruction of an actual event.

However, on entering the restaurant, the leading Russian gangster, although wielding a gun, establishes himself as physically dangerous by head-butting one of the gangsters seated at the restaurant table. The butt is sudden, swift and unexpected, whereas the gun play later in the sequence was signalled from the very opening shots. Asked what was the most violent part of the clip, the head-butt was singled out for attention on the grounds, 'that was quite unusual, you don't see that very often'. Asked was it realistic, the reply was, 'Fairly, yes'.

Although these young men may not have been familiar with machine pistols as a tool of injury, one could be certain that they were no strangers to the effectiveness of the head-butt as a technique for inflicting pain, and indeed when asked, 'What made it realistic?' replied, 'It sounded quite real'. The impression we gained was that these men enjoyed the head-butt scene and did so because it was unusual for such a drama, and also because it was an accurate depiction, through the effective use of sound, of a head-butt – something they were in a position to evaluate. Looking at the sequence as a whole and at their responses to it, this definitely fell into the category of violence with a little v. It is not clear whether it was little v because of the way the violence was shown, or because such forms of violence are now so common on television that it is no longer seen as strong violence. It may well be that the 'rules of injury' have moved to a point were the violence in *Thief Takers* can no longer be taken seriously.

Deep Cover: *depicted real violence*

Having established that *Thief Takers* was not very violent and required no editing, we then showed a sequence from the film, *Deep Cover*, where one of the members of a gang has talked to the police. The leader of the gang wreaks vengeance on the informer by clubbing him with a pool cue and repeatedly smashes his face until it is a bloody pulp. The rest of the gang look on in horror at the severity of the punishment. There is much blood, and at one point blood spurts from the victim's mouth.

Asked, 'How violent was that?', the answer was, 'You'd never see that on television'. (Two versions of *Deep Cover* were shown to the groups: an unedited film version, and a version edited for transmission by Carlton Television. At the time of writing, neither version has been shown.) As far as these young men were concerned, the unedited version was violence with a big V. Something defined as violent can nonetheless be enjoyed, and these men did indeed enjoy it. It was obvious that for most in this group the unedited version was the preferred one, and editing was undertaken to see which elements made this clip especially violent.

Where other groups altered *Deep Cover* by removing some of the direct action, and concentrating on the reactions of the witnesses, these young men, in the only scene they edited during the session, did the exact opposite. They removed the reaction shots and left only the violent blows to the body. The cinema version consists of a sequence of six blows, each one followed by various versions of the pained reactions of those forced to view the attack, unable to intervene. The version edited by Carlton had reduced the blows to three, concentrating on the reaction shots. The same strategy, with minor variations, was adopted by all the other groups who edited the scene.

But instead of reducing the number of blows and cushioning them with the intervening reaction shots, the 'hard' men edited a sequence of uninterrupted violence so that the six blows followed one after another.

Excitement of violence

Referring to the cinema version, one of these young men said:

> *It's more exciting. My girlfriend would rather watch a romantic film.*
> *I have to lock her in the car when I go to a video shop.*

These men viewed the world in rugged terms, but they possessed a strong sense of justice, and in judging any behaviour – on the screen or in real life – they thought in terms of whether or not it 'deserved a smack', without questioning whether 'a smack' was itself legitimate. Within rule-governed limits, violence was as natural to them as verbal reasoning might be to other people.

To these men the cinema version of *Deep Cover* was 'exciting', and the head-butting scene in *Thief Takers* was attractive because it was 'quite unusual'. Later we shall see that one or two of these young men had seen a video of real life executions, and although they found it 'sick', they enjoyed watching it.

This might explain this group's enjoyment of screen violence, but they were not alone in enjoying it. We asked what made *Deep Cover* violent:

> *The way it's made realistic – the blood. And the fact that he only hit him once and he fell over. Sometimes they get hit about 400 times and they still stand up.*

> *I think the shocked expressions of everyone standing by is realistic as well.*

Other groups felt that the onlookers' horror heightened the feeling of violenc in this clip. These men, however, had to see the blows, and they had to see blood, and the edit they made shows this.

These were the reactuoins when we ran the whole scene in black and white:

> *It's no different in black and white.*

> *It didn't look as good to me.*

We asked if the black and white version was as violent as the colour version:

> *It was exactly the same. I didn't notice the blood until you mentioned it anyway.*

The last comment referred to the shot of the blood spraying from the vistim's mouth. This was one of the shots that Carlton edited out, and while it was virtually impossible to see in black and white, it could be seen in colour, although easy to miss. The group preferred to see the blood in colour, but it was on aesthetic grounds:

> *It didn't look so good to me.*

Members of this group enjoyed the violence. The beating and the injuries sustained were believable: the victim was not able to get up after the first swipe with the cue. We pressed the issue of colour and once more took up the issue of blood.

> *It was still as violent but it didn't stand out as much in black and white.*

> *[Prompt] I would have thought the colour would have made it more violent?*

I think it was better in colour, yes. It was more gory.

We return to our earlier point: in many instances viewers define violence on the basis of cinematic rules of violence, not on the basis of experience. The slow motion death in *Schindlers' List* added to the perception of violence, or at least it did for these viewers, and the atmosphere of powerlessness and impending doom helped to make more violent what physical violence there was. One of these young men noted the powerlessness of the victims:

They got shot in the head when they were on their knees.

The Krays: *reality & authenticity*

This group of 'hard' young men were also shown the bio-drama of the Kray twins. Their reactions, and the terms they used, force us to consider again what the respondents mean by 'reality'. Do they mean that an act looks real because it corresponds to how an eye witness would see the act? Or do they mean that the screen act captures a feeling of being real?

The clip from the Kray film showed the Krays attacking a rival gang in a billiard hall. At one point a beating is given over a billiard table, and finally a sword is slowly pushed through the hand of one of the rival gang members. This group wanted no edits to be made and, although they considered it violent, did not accept that it was as violent as the previous pool room fight from *Deep Cover*. They did, however, consider that the Kray film 'looked more realistic'. The realism point was explored, and we asked members of the group to compare the two films for realism:

The Krays. Especially when he had him over the table and was punching him.

We noticed that during this scene some of the young men laughed, and asked:

[Prompt] What was realistic about that? You were laughing there.

It was a bit like a comedy.

This scene was not played for laughs. No-one in the other groups considered the scene amusing. What made these young men chuckle seems to have been the disorganised nature of the blows delivered as the Krays attempted to inflict injury on a body that was not positioned to best advantage. One would imagine it was the type of situation these men recognised as being 'true': real fist fighting is a rather 'scruffy' affair with little technical precision. In the pool room sequence from *Deep Cover* the assailant looks as if he knows what he is doing. By contrast the beating over the billiard table, although effective enough judging by the shouts of pain, appears a decidedly amateur attempt at injury, and hence the need for repeated blows, since no single blow found a ready mark for conclusive hurt.

These young men gauged the degree of violence of the fight by its realism. Indeed, it was the very reality of the scene that made it comic because in real life such fights can look absurd.

When we come to examine responses to a scene where a man is hit by an outraged citizen outside a court, we shall see that the clumsiness of a real punch produced amusement, and not just among this group of 'hard' men. A real act of violence does not have to look horrific to produce hurt, but to capture the hurt it has often to be made to look horrific. It is often this manufacturing of the 'real' by using horror and over-emphasisis that makes for violence with a big V.

The changing nature of violence

The action of the Kray film was seen as old-fashioned by this group. One of the respondents, comparing the two films, said of the Krays:

> It's a lot older. I think it was really violent in its day, but not now.

The sheer cleverness of modern special effects, and the commitment of film makers to ensuring that violence is presented in graphic detail, over-emphasises reality. To construct a violent act on film, using the close focus so often employed in modern films, is to slow it down, no matter at what speed it is shot. In real life, action is never viewed with such concentrated focus, and is usually over almost before it happens. The real violent act can be missed because of the sheer speed of the action, and it is only after the event that one reassembles what has occurred to provide an account of what has happened.

Even death as shown by the news – for example a Saigon policeman shooting a Vietcong suspect in the head, the first occasion that British news had used that type of footage – has a speed that is missing in the cinema. In the case of the Vietcong suspect, the bullet to the head, the falling to the ground, and the spurting of the blood, is over before one realises or constructs what has happened. Furthermore, the violence has not been set up. There is no lead up. It just happens almost out of the blue. Because cinema can linger over the details, fictional violence has become a yardstick by which to judge non-fictional violence.

The ability to capture, almost with a clinician's eye, the details of an injury, gives film violence a new status. It suggests that film violence is researched violence; that it depicts violence as it is, rather than as the product of the film maker's craft in the pursuit of dramatic impact. Yet the thought remains — and there is evidence for this from all the edit groups — that the new rules of film violence have created a feeling that people understand violence through personal experience. Such a statement would have been impossible to make about an audience fed on the violence of Randolph Scott, or even Matt Dillon.

In spite of this, there is still no serious confusion between the real and the fictional. For example, one respondent criticised the scene in *Pulp Fiction* where Marvin, a back seat passenger in a car driven by his 'abductors', accidentally has his head blown apart by a shot fired from the front seat. It was seen as incredible that the trajectory of the blood and brains would be forward to the front seat, and not backwards to cover the rear window.

Nevertheless, the constant reference by respondents to the 'reality' of the violence in dramatic production suggests that one outcome of the new rules of injury has been a definition of violence that applies only to fiction. The 'new rules' have created a 'false knowledge' of violence.

We shall return to discuss the influence of screen violence on definitions of violence, but it is worth noting that to witness real life violence is different from witnessing screen violence, and to witness real life screen violence is different from witnessing fictional screen violence. Each engages the emotions differently. What we need to explore now is the part that emotional involvement plays in defining violence. We can do this in an area close to people's lives — domestic violence.

Domestic violence as authentic violence

By looking at domestic violence we can again consider the divide between fictional and non-fictional violence. Although not always hidden, domestic violence is nevertheless submerged, in that no more than a fraction of it becomes publicly known. Furthermore, as with rape, domestic violence is not always easy to define.

Of all the clips shown, those featuring domestic violence produced perhaps the strongest responses, and not just from women. Indeed, some men appeared more outraged than the women. This is violence close to home, and domestic violence is universally viewed with distaste.

We showed the group a clip of domestic violence taken from *Brookside*, and a clip from *Ladybird, Ladybird*, a powerful drama of domestic violence by Ken Loach. None of these 'hard' young men approved of the behaviour they saw, but in the course of the discussion that followed the Ken Loach clip, one respondent said:

> *In my opinion if a woman's strong enough to stand up to a man, she's strong enough to take a chinning.*

Such a view is unlikely to find general support, but the comment had an old fashioned gallantry to it, implying that women are weak and to be protected. Women were to be harmed only if they 'stood out of line'.

Primary definers

Domestic violence is close to home, and allows us to see where everyday social values influence definitions of screen violence. We saw this in every group, and not just among these 'hard' men.

We showed first the scene from *Brookside* where the husband turns on his wife. The police arrive, having been alerted by the neighbours, but are turned away by the wife under instructions from the husband to convince them that nothing is wrong. Following the departure of the police the husband takes his fury out on his wife. We will run the discussion as it appears direct from the transcript.

This is from *Brookside* – it was a running story line where the mother and daughter killed the father and buried him under the patio.

I only watched it because of that.

[Prompt] So you normally don't watch it?

No, but I thought it would be good.

[Prompt] We showed the wife-beating scene, and asked: 'Was that violent?'

No.

[Prompt] You don't see anything do you?

I thought the sound was quite violent.

Yes, it was just the noise. Nothing else was violent.

[Prompt] Why — what was missing?

You didn't actually see the punch.

[Prompt] So, the violence is the act?

You've got to see the act to make it violent, yes.

[Prompt] But the sound can make it more realistic?

Yes.

[Prompt] Have you ever seen any violence that you haven't been able to look at?

At the cinema, yes.

[Prompt] You've seen the Kray film — when he puts the knife into Jack the Hat's eye, did you feel squeamish about that?

It's just a film isn't it?

If you saw it in real life you'd probably throw up.

[Prompt] OK we're going to lower the sound so you hear some thumps . . . in real life when you see a glassing does the person scream?

Everyone just moves out the way. The person being glassed usually shouts.

[Prompt] OK, let's see this with the sound taken down . . . would you say that was violent?

No, not at all. You have to leave the sound in to make it at all violent. It's only the sound that makes it violent.

The sound makes the scene doesn't it?

From this, a few principles can be established about defining violence. These young men did not consider *Brookside* to be violent with a big V. The first principle, therefore, is that violence with a big V must involve witnessing the violent act. Creating an impression of violence is not enough. Yet it would appear that sound can make a scene violent – 'It was just the noise. Nothing else was violent'. And indeed one did not witness the blows to the man's wife, only heard the thud of his fist.

This group did not ask to edit the *Brookside* clip. The edit that was made, or rather discussed – lowering the sound – explored the role of sound in violence. These young men are true to the principle that for something to be violent, the act must be seen. What they appear to be saying is that sound adds to the violence, without being in itself violence. But it is a close call. The relative importance of action and sound was explored more fully in the second clip, from *Lady Bird, Lady Bird*.

Swearing as violence

In this sequence the husband sits waiting for his wife to return from shopping. He is drinking beer, getting agitated, and explodes in fury when his wife returns because her lateness shows a lack of respect for him. His temper is ferocious, and the violence savage. Fists and feet are used in the assault, accompanied by a serious verbal onslaught. Again, we will run through the transcript of the responses. We asked: 'How violent was that'?

Definitely more violent

You still didn't see him punching her but it was a lot more violent.

You see him kicking her, you hear shouting and swearing.

[Prompt] Can you have verbal violence? He kept calling her 'cunt' all the time didn't he?

There are some swear words that are worse than others.

Normally it would be cow or something.

I don't think I've ever heard that word on television before.

No, it's very unusual.

[Prompt] Would you keep the 'C' word in there?

Yes, it made the scene. You don't ever hear that on television.

[Prompt] Did you find that type of violence stronger than the pool room violence [Deep Cover] you saw?

Yes, I do.

[Prompt] Why?

It's a lot more real.

I think it's worse because it's a man beating up a woman.

[Prompt] That makes it more violent, does it?

Yes.

[Prompt] He completely loses it, doesn't he?

You can tell he's going to lose it by the way he's breathing, but I wouldn't have thought he would have lost it that much.

What is interesting here is the technical way the film is discussed – not technical in the sense of film criticism, but technical in terms of studying human behaviour. There is keen attention to the man's breathing as a sign – 'you can tell he's going to lose it' – but even this respondent was surprised that 'he would have lost it that much'. We said earlier that violence is exciting because it offers a break with the mundane, and in these comments there is almost a connoisseur's discussion of the use of the 'C' word. They are fascinated by its appearance on television – 'it's very unusual' – but its inclusion is approved, even enjoyed – the 'C' word 'made the scene. You don't ever hear that on television.'

Members of this group probably themselves used the word cunt, but the approval with which it was greeted suggests the enjoyment of difference. That is, like violence itself, it was exciting because it broke with the expected.

Anyone viewing *Ladybird, Ladybird* would declare it violent, but it is interesting that these 'hard' young men found it more violent than *Deep Cover*, which was certainly more bloody. They defined *Ladybird, Ladybird* as more violent because it was considered 'a lot more real', although *Deep Cover* had also been described as realistic. Indeed, the beating that took place in *Deep Cover* was judged true to the situation in its setting. The fact that *Ladybird, Ladybird* was held to be more real – and more violent – must be accounted for by the fact that such violence really does happen, and happens in their own world. In other words, the violence had an authenticity which was absent from *Deep Cover*.

Domestic violence is authentic violence because it involves relationships that we all know, even though we may not all engage in domestic violence. Authentic violence is close violence, and for that reason uncomfortable. Furthermore, it is wrong violence. The violence of *Deep Cover* might be expected among those who live outside the law, where people must enforce order and obedience without recourse to the law.

This is not so with domestic violence, which is not only wrong, but shameful. The violence in *Deep Cover* is professional violence, while the violence in *Ladybird, Ladybird* is not. It is worth noting that one of the young men thought the domestic violence stronger 'because it is a man beating up a woman' – a scene is more readily defined as violent if there is an unequal distribution of power. It may be because of unequal physical strength between the sexes, but it can also be due to the inability of someone to protect himself and fight back. The helplessness of one party, in other words, increases the likelihood that a scene will be defined as violent.

There is, then, with these young men a sense of injustice in their perception of the *Ladybird, Ladybird* scene. These respondents were not shy of violence, but, to them, attacking a woman as in this clip is not masculine. It is an unfair contest with no risk to the self. Even if these young men might 'smack' a woman who stepped out of line, the comment, 'I wouldn't have thought he would have lost it that much', implies that the violence was excessive.

Status of the victim

We wanted to find out if the conduct of the victim might influence the definition of violence. We put it to this group: 'What if the woman in that scene had been having a go at him, calling him useless in bed etc, and really winding him up – would it have made it less violent'?

> *It wouldn't have made it less violent but you'd have thought he had more reason to do it.*

> *If she had hit him first it would have been less violent.*

Yes, purely because of the fact that she started it. He would have had more reason to hit her back. If it was two men no-one would be shocked. It does make it more violent because it's a woman. But if she had hit him first it would have made it less violent.

It's a lot worse seeing a woman get hit than seeing a bloke get hit.

We asked the group what their response would be, 'If you saw a bouncer outside a club hitting a young lad?'

That wouldn't be out of order the way I look at it. If the young lad got completely pissed in the club the bouncer would only be doing his job. He's there to stop people getting hurt. If the kid hit the bouncer then why shouldn't he hit him back?

The response was unequivocal, so we asked:

But what if he'd hit a woman or a much older man?

It would have been more violent.

Moral judgement

These young men considered the domestic violence in *Ladybird, Ladybird* to be very violent; it was violent because the violence was seen as 'real'; it was seen as real because it was authentic. It involved a physically weak woman and a physically strong man – it was unfair. It was unfair also because the woman had done nothing to deserve the beating. Clearly, moral judgement has a role to play in deciding – at least among these young men – levels of violence, and even whether a scene is violent at all.

For these young men to invoke moral considerations is not surprising. In real life they had to decide who was sufficiently 'out of order' to deserve 'a smack', but even the administration of violence follows rules: it has to be a reasonably fair contest.

This point was well illustrated by a documentary on bear baiting in India, a *Channel 4 Special*. In the film bears are chained to a stake, teeth pulled and claws blunted so as not to hurt the dogs, which are then released to bait the bears. Responses following the film were immediate and offered before the moderator had put any questions to them:

It's out of line that is.

It's sick isn't it?

I'd like to see a big bear come in and kill all the Pakis.

When asked if the film was violent there was total agreement that it was. Someone said:

Violence normally involves humans. That was just out of order.

When asked, 'If that was two bears in the wild fighting over a mate would that be violent?' the reply was:

No, because it's nature.

For something to be natural appears to make it right, and what is right in that context cannot be violent. Violence, it would seem, has to involve humans, and the bear baiting was not just violent but 'sick'. It was men who had structured an event that would not otherwise have occurred in the form it did. Unfairness is never far from the surface of the definition of the violence. Asked, 'What if the bear hadn't had its teeth and claws taken out?', the opinion was:

It wouldn't be as bad. That's just totally unfair.

We asked if the scenes shown were enjoyable to watch:

No, it's like bullfighting. I went to see a bullfight and I didn't like it.

His lack of enjoyment stemmed from its being, in his opinion, 'unfair'. Somebody else also had seen a bullfight and had failed to enjoy it:

You just know the bull is not going to stand a chance.

One must be careful to separate defining something as violent from the enjoyment of violence, and these young men did enjoy watching violence. For example, it was put to one of the respondents who said he had seen a video of a real life execution· 'If there was a video of cock fighting and bear baiting would you get that out'? He replied:

I'd watch it, yes.

and then added:

There are some scenes with animals in that video on executions. There is a scene where a group of people are sitting at a table and they bring in a monkey in the cage and they all take turns in hitting it with a hammer until it dies. It can't go anywhere and it just spins round and round.

Asked about his reaction to the scene, he said:

It's just sick again isn't it?'.

We asked whether, had he known the video included such a scene, he would have taken it out of the shop. He replied: 'Yes, I would'. This prompted us to ask: 'Is there any type of violence that you wouldn't watch?', to which we received a firm, 'No'.

After watching news footage of injuries sustained in a bomb attack, we asked the whole group whether or not they had ever 'seen anything on the news that you've had to turn your head away from?' There was general agreement that this had never occurred, but it was at this point that the respondent who had watched the video of a monkey being hammered to death recalled something else he had seen:

I've seen a film called Executions *which was banned as soon as it came out. The last scene in that where a guy gets shot in the head makes you feel ill. When you see it you can see why it was banned. It was disgusting.*

Disgusting or not, someone else in the group admitted: 'I've seen it a few times'. Pressed for the attraction of watching such material, he replied:

I don't know really. He deserved it anyway so it didn't bother me. I think people who kill other people should get killed.

For these men, the idea of culpability alters the whole way scenes of violence are viewed.

If he was innocent, say he'd just robbed a shop, then yes, that would make a difference.

The idea of robbing a shop as innocent behaviour may seem surprising, but we take it that he means such behaviour would not warrant execution. It is difficult to be sure, but maybe the execution would have been regarded as more violent if he had simply robbed a shop than if he had killed someone.

One wonders how enjoyable the viewing of such material can be. If it were not enjoyable then it would not have been viewed repeatedly, but, as if to explain himself, he said:

I only watched it because my mate had it. There's all different things on it, it's not just people getting shot... Everyone has their fascination and curiosity.

It would seem that, for this group, even if something was 'sick' or very violent it did not mean it could not be enjoyed, and that the violence was an integral part of the enjoyment. Violence, death and injury intrigued these young men, and, as we will see from the other groups, they were not alone in this.

Real life death & injury

We showed the group news footage to see at what point images were held to be violent. We showed scenes from Sarajevo broadcast on Croatian television, but not in Britain. We also showed unedited footage of a cafe in Sarajevo when a mortar bomb exploded close by. In the unedited footage there is a shot of a man's headless body, and of a woman's body being carried to a truck in which the head is so tenuously attached to the body that it looks as if the tissue keeping it attached might tear at any moment and sever the head completely. Asked if this news footage was violent, the reply was negative:

> *You haven't actually seen the act of violence. You've only seen the end result. Obviously it's real and it makes you feel sorry for them. You know that person being dragged along is actually dead, it's not just a film. But I wouldn't say it's violent because you don't see any violence.*

Other comments given were: 'It was gory', and, 'It was sick'. Asked how it was sick, the response was: 'That shot with the head hanging off'. We took up the point that it was not violent because one never actually saw the action that caused the carnage: 'Was it not violent because you didn't see any action'?

> *I don't know if it's the sort of thing you'd want to see any action in. I don't know if you'd want to see a bomb actually being dropped. If it was on the news you'd watch it, but I don't think you'd go and rent out a film to watch people being blown up.*

Asked if he was upset by the pictures, he said he was: 'The fact that it's real – nothing is staged'. So real violence was upsetting, or the consequences of violence were upsetting, in a way that, for this group, fictional violence wass not upsetting.

News is viewed differently from fictional violence. To see the explosion would have made the scenes very violent, but would it have added anything to the story? The story was that people had been killed and injured by a bomb, not that this is how bombs land and explode. We asked this group, 'If you were an editor would you put that on?' They responded:

> As long as it was late and kids weren't still up, I'd put it on so people can see what is going on.

> I think anything like that would be positive – it would make people aware.

In other words, the news has a point and purpose to it.

Violence must be seen

As we have seen, in fiction this group felt they had to see action for the scene to be perceived as violent – the aftermath of violence was not enough. But it was different with factual material. We showed them news footage from the 1970s which had recently been used in a documentary about the IRA. In the clip shown there is a massive bang and the noise of falling masonry and shattering glass as a bomb goes off in a town shopping area. A child is heard crying and may possibly be hurt, but it is difficult to say. We asked if this was violence, and the answer was:

> Yes, you're watching violence.

> It's the sound again. If you didn't have that soundtrack it wouldn't seem half as violent.

As we saw earlier, sound isn't violent on its own, but it can add to the sense of violence. We asked whether this scene was as disturbing as the Sarajevo pictures:

> No, I would say that wasn't nearly as bad as that.

> There are no injuries here – they even said themselves that no-one was killed.

Thus, for something to be disturbing it does not have to be violent, and violence is not necessarily disturbing.

It is only rarely that the news captures violence at the moment it takes place. The action is usually over by the time a camera crew is in position to film, although very occasionally a crew may stumble across violence in progess. We wondered how this group would respond to violence filmed as it happened. The scene we showed was a punch thrown at an Italian man outside the court where he had just been convicted for stealing a teddy bear from the pile of tributes left outside Kensington Palace as a mark of respect to Princess Diana.

Before asking about the pictures, we needed to establish their response to Princess Diana's death. We felt that this might colour their reaction to this clip.

We began the sequence, therefore, by asking: 'When Princess Di was killed, were you upset at all?'

It was weird. She was all over the papers and all of a sudden she's dead and we don't really know what happened.

[Prompt] But what was your reaction? Were you sad?

I wasn't really sad. The thing is you don't know her. It's not like one of your family dying, is it?

You could drop dead and you wouldn't get a mention in your local paper.

Dodi died in the car as well and he hardly got a mention, did he?

We thought that even had they been upset they might not like to confess to such 'soft' emotions, and so we approached the question from a different direction to see if there was any sign that they had been moved to sadness. We asked: 'What about your girlfriends, were they upset?' They said they were, but comfort was not forthcoming from these men.

It was a good excuse to go out on the day of the funeral – all the roads were quiet.

My girlfriend was upset. She cried. I just told her to shut up.

Princess Diana's death, then, did not seem to upset these respondents unduly. The first of two clips of the assault on the Italian was shown. This was unedited and featured an extremely drunk Scotsman, who had difficulty in keeping his feet and who slurred his words incomprehensibly in a thick accent. He kept interjecting while the Italian was being interviewed to camera, offered vulgar abuse, and accused the man of 'mugging my Diana'. He made a final stagger to the Italian and swung a punch to the side of his head. Amazingly, it connected, and the Italian, who did not see it coming, was clearly hurt and shocked.

Immediately the clip was over, one of the young men said: 'Brilliant'. Asked why it was brilliant, he replied:

> *Yes, I was pleased he got done. Anyone who steals off a grave should get done, not just because it was her.*

Asked if it was violent, the responses were:

> *No, but it was realistic.*

> *It was funny.*

We then showed the transmitted version. In this much shorter version the Italian is being interviewed and, without any explanation, the Scotsman is beside the Italian and throws the punch. The sound of the punch is louder in this version because the noise of the traffic has been reduced by editing. On technical grounds, the punch met with approval:

> *It's just a classic punch in the side of the head.*

Asked which version was more violent, the agreement was:

> *The second one because it looks as if he's just walked straight up to him and punched him in the face.*

> *In the first one you knew he was going to do it. You were ready for it.*

> *You hardly ever see a punch like that because the person knows it's coming. He didn't know it was coming because he was too interested in talking to the cameras. He didn't know it was going to happen.*

> *The sound was realistic.*

A few points are worth noting. The unedited version is not considered violent, although it clearly contains an act of violence. It was seen as 'funny', and, as we shall see shortly, what is funny is rarely considered violent, even though the injury inflicted may be graphic. Why this should be so is not difficult to understand. Violence has negative consequences: in extreme cases it results in death, and in all cases means injury and pain, so to be hurt is not funny. Conversely, if something is funny, it is not violence. In the unedited version, because the scene was funny, it was difficult to take the violence seriously. The Scotsman was not merely drunk, but falling-down drunk, and the scene was thus comic. In the edited version – the one considered more violent – the blow is delivered more professionally. It no longer appears as a drunken swing, but as a purposeful jab. The only explanation of why the punch was thrown is from the story, namely that a passer-by hit the foreigner because he stole a teddy bear from the tributes to Princess Di, and we are not told that the assailant was drunk. At first we thought that the two scenes were taken by two different cameras, but that is not the case. Close examination reveals that it is the same take, but that the sound of the traffic has been lowered in the second, making the contact between fist and head louder, and the punch, which is somewhat feeble, appears more focused, direct and powerful. In addition, the punch comes as a surprise, increasing its shock value.

Comedy is not violence

The final clip shown to this group was a scene from *Pulp Fiction* where two 'enforcers' for an underworld gang go to an apartment to collect money that a group of young men should have handed over to the boss of the gang, but have kept for themselves. The young men are killed, except for one who is taken for a ride in the enforcers' car. The mood shifts, and there is a discussion which has all the marks of three friends amiably chatting, when a gun goes off, accidentally shooting the young man in the rear seat, and splattering the contents of his head over the two in the front of the car. Asked if that was violent, the responses were:

> *No, it was funny.*
>
> *They're joking about it, it takes the edge off the violence.*
>
> *You don't actually see any violence do you?*

The young man who is killed is called Marvin. Immediately following the discharge of the gun his killer says in absolute surprise: 'I've just shot Marvin in the face'. He does not say 'head', but 'face'. What makes the scene funny – and nearly all respondents in the group fixed on this – was, 'I've just shot Marvin in the face': the cosy familiarity of the scene; the use of the young man's first name; 'face' instead of 'head'.

Whatever the attraction of screen violence – and these 'hard' young men were certainly attracted – violence itself is subverted by humour. To test the power of humour we used video editing techniques. We took a clip that had already been defined by these respondents as violent, *Deep Cover*, and overlaid the scenes with laughter taken from a comedy sketch. When blows of the pool cue were delivered, and the camera cut to the responses of the on-lookers, it was accompanied by gales of laughter. It was agreed:

That was funny.

It's like Natural Born Killers where there is a scene where a father is touching up his daughter in a kind of American sitcom spoof way.

Asked specifically if it was now funny and not violent, the response was:

Yes, it made me laugh.

I thought it was funny.

Someone else added a more lengthy observation:

If that was a programme on television and they were laughing and joking about something beforehand and everyone is laughing while he's getting beaten up and they're still laughing afterwards then it's going to be funny — exactly the same as Pulp Fiction.

Another voice offered:

No, I wouldn't say so [violent] because it's like comedy. You wouldn't think it was violent. You wouldn't be standing there laughing, would you?

3

Ruff, Tuff 'n' Streetwise

The next group – the 'hard women', aged between 18 and 24 - were recruited on the same basis as the 'hard men'. They were not the exact female equivalent of the men, but were all familiar with violence in real life.

Experience of violence

'Hard' they may have been, but whereas their male counterparts claimed the type of television they liked was 'action' and 'Arnold Schwarzenegger and Steven Seagal' (as well as a range of other programmes – the *Fast Show* was mentioned for example) these women, unprompted, simply listed their favourite soap operas, programmes that were not even mentioned by the 'hard' men.

In common with the men, most of the violence they had witnessed was associated with drink, but violence had been experienced on the street, where, as one woman put it, she had 'gobbed others off'. They were asked, 'Has anyone been really frightened [by violence]?'

> *It depends who's involved, whether it's a friend or relation who is being threatened.*

> *I think the adrenalin kicks in.*

We asked if they found such situations exciting:

> *Not exiting, no.*

> *It depends how bad it is – if it's just people mucking around you tend to have a look to see what's going on, but if it's a big fight that breaks out you tend to back off.*

If it's nothing to do with you then you don't get involved but if it's your friends you've got to because you can't leave your friends.

If a group of girls jumped on my friends you couldn't just stand there and watch them getting beaten up.

We asked whether they seen anything on television they 'thought was too violent'. Although not able to recall the film, one person said:

I couldn't watch parts of that — it was chopping off people's legs and severing their heads and things — that is just a bit too graphic.

Others claimed not to have seen material that they considered too violent:

No, because when films are shown on TV they usually cut half of it out anyway.

[Prompt] Does that annoy you?

Yes. If you've seen something at the cinema and it then comes on television and you think you'd like to watch it again you think, 'well, where's this bit and that bit?' More often than not they're the best bits.

Intrigued by the idea of 'the best bit', we pressed for explanation of 'best'. 'More action', she replied. Once more we see violence equated with pace.

Thief Takers: *a lack of belief*

The first clip we showed was *Thief Takers*. As with the 'hard' men, no-one considered it really violent. One woman made the same point that had been made by their male counterparts: 'You expect things like that nowadays on TV'. Another respondent went so far as to say:

I thought it was quite amusing actually, especially that bit where the guy told him to sit down and he nutted him.

Taken as a whole, the scene was viewed as unrealistic, and the violence of a type that fails to engage the viewer. When asked if it was realistic, one woman replied:

I don't know — I've never been in one.

Of course there is no need to have been in a situation to understand the inappropriateness of behaviour:

The police would be in full body armour for a start, not just in little baseball caps like that – they'd have big shields over the faces and they wouldn't have little guns like that, they'd have big rifles.

There would be more police if they knew the guys inside had guns.

We wanted to know whether the dramatic device of having death played out in slow motion increased the sense of violence. One respondent said most emphatically, 'No', but this prompted the comment from another participant:

It's just trying to emphasise what's going on – it's trying to get you to watch it a bit more closely when it's going slower.

Someone else added:

I suppose it has a bit more of an impact when it's going slower.

They agreed the film could be broadcast before the nine o'clock watershed. According to one participant, it was not 'the sort of violence where you're cringing. It doesn't make you squeamish or jumpy.' Again, we see that for something to be violent in any strong sense it must break the rhythm of the normal. At some point violence must give a cognitive jolt.

Deep Cover: *shock of the unexpected*

We moved on quickly to show the poolroom scene from *Deep Cover*.

I think that was far worse than the first one.

Yes, begging for mercy. It was mindless violence.

There was more blood in it as well.

When they get shot it's a quick death, but that was a painful death.

And with people just watching.

[Prompt] When you watch violence like that are you more involved – does it hold your attention more?

The reply was a definite, 'Yes'.

[Prompt] But why?

It made me jump.

[Prompt] What was the thing that was violent?

The fact that he was begging for mercy, and he just carried on.

It was a lot more physical than the one before.

Having caught the audience's attention through violence, the beating is then remorseless, but more than that, the victim, so badly damaged by the first blow, is helpless to fight back and can only lie on the pool table moaning and pleading for mercy. It is the helplessness of the victim that heightens the sense of violence. Violence is more likely to be defined when there is an unequal distribution of power. This scene was also held to be a lot more physical than the scene in *Thief Takers*: the injury was delivered at close quarters by a pool cue, and injury was protracted, not swift:

> *When they get shot it's a quick death, but that was a painful death.*

The portrayal of pain undoubtedly ratchets up the violence, and the fact that the victim pleaded for mercy adds to itsthe emotional intensity. Through the reactions of others around the table who look away and beseech the boss of the gang to stop the beating, the audience are being asked to will the punishment to stop. In a sense, one is a participant in this violence.

Feelings are involved

The fact that the victim 'was begging for mercy, and he just carried on' undoubtedly had an emotional effect on this group, but only up to a point. We asked, 'What was the thing that was violent?'

> *Depends on what the guy has done — for all we know he might deserve it.*
>
> *[Prompt] What if he had raped and mutilated the bloke's wife, would that make it less violent, if you knew that beforehand?*
>
> *You wouldn't feel so sorry for him.*

Empathy with the victim appeared to play a part in the definition of violence, and another principle is thus established: the more a character is liked and known, the less 'objective' violence is needed for it to be seen as violence. In soap operas, for example, a lower level of violence is perceived as violence with a big V, because the audience has lived with the characters for a long time, and feels that it knows them as 'real people'.

Realism is not 'the real'

Violent as they found *Deep Cover* to be, they didn't find it as bad as real life violence. In general, a diet of screen violence doesn't seem to lessen the shock of violence in real life. The two types of violence are experienced entirely differently. One member of this group had seen someone 'glassed':

I was standing at the bar and a group of lads who'd had too much to drink just started fighting and then they just started picking up things and throwing them at each other. One of them just picked up a bottle and smashed it in another lad's face.

Asked to compare this with screen violence, she said:

When you see it with your own eyes and it's for real of course it's realistic. When you see it on TV they try to make it realistic, but it's never the same as when you see it with your own eyes.

On the whole these 'hard' young women didn't want to edit the clip, but when asked to do so with a view to lowering the impact of the violence, they made the following comments. The spray of blood from the man's mouth was considered by one woman, 'very effective', on the grounds that it was not 'expected', but another woman said that she had enjoyed the clip except for, 'where there was a spray of blood where they hit him at one point'. A third woman said:

I think they have to have that in because you can't go around hitting someone with a baseball bat and nothing happens.

In other words, the spray of blood signified a serious beating, although there were certainly enough other signs to get the message across. And there were other comments:

I think they could cut that spraying of blood — they could just have him covered in blood.

I wouldn't make it so loud.

The issue of the watershed was raised without prompting, which helped us to focus the discussion on what counts as violence:

I think if you were cutting it for being shown before nine o'clock you could take out quite a few of the beatings and focus more on the people around watching.

This we did, retaining the sound, but cutting the actual blows. The story was told by the expressions of the on-lookers. The group agreed, 'It's not as gory', but it was still held to be too powerful for showing before nine o'clock. Someone else said, 'I'd take out the first scream'. It was also agreed that the swearing that accompanied the beating 'made it more realistic'. Edits were duly made, but the conclusion was: 'I don't think it made any difference'. We then showed the version edited by Carlton, which was fairly close to the edit that this group had made:

Yes, that's what I said — they've taken the violence out and focused more on the people around.

You only see one or two [violent] shots.

Asked if the version they had made was more violent than Carlton's version, it was agreed that theirs was more violent.

Their version was more violent than the one edited by Carlton because they enjoyed the violence, and therefore could not reduce the violence too far without disappointing their appetite for action. Asked which version of all the versions they preferred, the response was, 'the violent one', meaning the unedited version, on the grounds that, 'it's more interesting'. We followed this by asking, 'would you like to see more violence than that?' 'Yes', was one response, 'it wouldn't bother me', to which someone added, 'It doesn't frighten me'.

Basically these young women had a high degree of tolerance to screen violence, and even enjoyed it. It was exiting. They defined violence as action. Seeing the blows, the instrument of injury, the consequences of action — blood on the face and the spray of blood from the mouth — these were the defining factors. Other factors, such as the reactions on the faces of the on-lookers, the noise of the blows, the screams and the pleading, enhanced it, but the central definition of violence arose from witnessing the acual injury — violence has to happen, and not simply be alluded to.

Domestic violence and personal involvement

Given that these young women appeared to take screen violence in their stride, and that they found the full version of *Deep Cover* 'more interesting' than the edited version, we decided to move straight on to the strong domestic violence of *Ladybird, Ladybird*. We wanted to know if that violence made for easy viewing, and if not, why not.

Having shown the clip, we asked simply, 'How would you describe that violence?'

Awful.

Disgusting.

Sad.

Although fictional, this film was judged by a different set of criteria from *Deep Cover*. We followed up the description, 'sad', and asked why:

The kids.

It's awful to think that sort of thing does actually go on.

It's awful to think that women put up with it as well. You just want to go and tell her to move out and leave him.

Clearly, for these women there was a different involvement in this drama than there was in *Deep Cover*. One participant confessed to having seen the whole film and said:

I was really crying most of the way through it.

The question is, is this film more violent than the violence in *Deep Cover*? After all, apart from one punch to the face – admittedly a very powerful blow – and some kicking, there is little direct contact and certainly no blood spraying from the mouth or indeed blood of any sort. The answer was, Yes. In contrast with *Deep Cover*, no-one wanted it to be more violent. Basically there was no enjoyment to be extracted from this violence, whereas the violence in *Deep Cover* was violence as excitement. As one woman said in relation to *Ladybird, Ladybird*:

I didn't really like watching it, but it does happen doesn't it?

We asked if they knew anyone who had been a victim of domestic violence:

I know a woman who lives down the street to my mum and the police are always round there.

We asked if there was any point in editing this sequence:

Well, they're trying to get a point across, they're trying to tell a story and how it really is – this is what happens in real life. You don't often hear of cases where men are beaten up by a baseball bat but a woman in a domestic violence situation – it happens all quite a lot.

Although the violence in *Deep Cover* was realistic, the setting was so removed from their own existence that it was not real. The violence in *Ladybird, Ladybird* involved them as people who might become involved in such violence. To leave the cinema after watching *Deep Cover* is to leave that world of violence behind; to leave the cinema after watching *Ladybird, Ladybird* is to re-enter the very world where that violence occurs:

> *The first type* [Deep Cover] *you know isn't real, but this type of thing you know goes on.*

There was discussion about whether you could tell if a man was likely to be violent towards women:

> *No, I think they are usually good at hiding it.*
> *I think a lot of them don't mean to do it — it's just jealousy.*
> *The quiet ones are often the worst. Sometimes someone who has been controlled all their life wants to have someone to beat up so they feel in control.*

Our efforts to make it less violent through editing met with resistance:

> *You couldn't edit that because it's the whole point of the story. It's showing what she's going through. I think like you said, the second bit where he's beating her is worse.*
> *He actually goes back and does it again instead of stopping and walking away.*
> *I don't know if you can edit it — it's the way the film is made.*

The film was editd by other groups. These women felt that the power of the scene draws its strength from the totality of the proceedings — it is act after act that makes it violent.

What shocked them was the sudden resurgence of violence. Just when they assumed it to be over, he returned to give his wife another beating as if the first had not been sufficient. Acts that continue longer than necessary to subdue the victim are classified as violent, and we see this throughout the general discussion of violence: repetitive violence is much stronger than quick violence. As one of the women observed: 'I think it makes it more dramatic when he goes back and does it again and again'. We said, 'Let's watch it again'. Having viewed the scene once more the repetitive nature of the violence was again commented on:

> He *actually goes back and does it again instead of stopping and walking away.*
> It's *the viciousness — she is really scared.*
> She's *just sitting there and taking it. You could see she was really scared.*

We can add another component to the definition of violence: 'viciousness'. And viciousness would seem to mean taking advantage of a powerless victim, and meting out violence that bears no relation to the 'offence' — if any.

Bad language as violence

The man uses a lot of strong language. It is aimed directly at the woman. He calls her a cunt more than once. We asked: 'Can language itself be violent?'

> *Yes.*
> [Prompt] *It's emotional abuse isn't it?*
> *Like you were saying at the beginning about 'gobbing off' — that can be violent, it doesn't have to be physical.*

This is an interesting contradiction of what they said before about one needing to see the act of hurt for something to be defined as violent.

> [Prompt] *There is a lot of bad language in* Pulp Fiction *though, isn't there?*
> *Yes, but I think it's that word.*
> *It's the 'C' word I don't like.*

In special circumstances, and by use of taboo words, language can be violence. It is possible that breaking strongly held linguistic taboos implies that other taboos will follow — eg hitting a woman — and we shall see some support for this later. For someone to be called a cunt, as in this film, is to show that the individual thus addressed has fallen to a level of no value in the eyes of the abuser, and that other behaviour, of a physical kind, will follow. The use of such a proscribed word also instils fear. In that sense, language can be seen as assault, even though no physical hurt is inflicted.

Nevertheless, although language can constitute violence in special circumstances, the general principle of violence is that physical force must be present. Throughout the beating the woman's two children watch from the kitchen, and although this added to the emotiveness of the scene, it did not serve to make it more violent:

> *I think what upset me the most when I watched it was seeing how upset the kids were.*

We asked it they wanted to edit the shots of the children:

> *Maybe some of it — they were actually watching their mum being beaten up.*
> *It wouldn't be as bad if the kids weren't there — maybe if they just heard it but didn't see it.*

Not all agreed:

> *It's more dramatic for this sort of scene to have them watching it.*

The conclusion, however, was:

> *It wouldn't be as emotional, but it would still be violent.*

Clearly, the children added enormously to the impact of the scene. Whether violence will disturb the viewer or not owes much to similar dramatic devices, but of themselves these devices do not affect whether a scene is defined as violent.

Violence, even strong violence, does not have to be upsetting, and for something to be defined as violent, even strong violence, does not necessarily mean it will not be enjoyed or found acceptable. For example, it may be acceptable to have a single scene in a film so violent that for some people it teeters on the edge of the unwatchable, but nevertheless is accepted providing the film does not contain such moments throughout. But we are not here interested in what is and what is not acceptable: such questions concern taste and values.

Aftermath of violence

An act is most easily perceived as violent if you witness the moment of injury. Much news does not count as violent, even though the scenes shown by the news are often harrowing. We showed this group of women the market bombing in Sarajevo, broadcast by Croatian television. When asked if this was violent, their answers were remarkably similar to their male counterparts:

No, it's not violent, it's more upsetting.

No, I think if we'd seen the actual bomb then it would be, but this is the aftermath.

It isn't violent — violence is where you actually see people being hurt. It's more emotional — you can't believe it's happened.

This is more people caring for each other after the violence. The violence is when it actually happens.

All these young women found the scene upsetting:

This is real life so it's more upsetting [than fiction] — you think of the families and everything. When you watch a violent film you know it's not real.

They thought that such graphic destruction ought not to be shown on the news:

I think they should show the relatives and the hospital, but I don't think the rest of it needs to be shown.

Why not?

Well it depresses people. It's not like you've just watched a film with lots of violence in it — that's actually happened.

We mentioned that, 'These things do go on', but that of itself was not seen as a warrant for showing such horror:

Yes, but you still know it's happened. It's more effective to show what's happened — it makes people think more, but I don't think it's necessary to actually show it.

This clip shocked and disturbed the group, but their response to showing real wounds in full detail was in line with findings from other studies conducted by the Leeds Institute: they did not want the camera to dwell on injuries.

In this group there was no confusion between real violence and cinematic violence, no matter how 'real' the fictional violence. There was one dissenting voice who found fictional violence more disturbing. Comparing the poolroom scene in *Deep Cover* with the devastated market-place in Sarajevo, one woman said:

I didn't feel squeamish by the woman's head but that spray of blood I couldn't stand... I think when you're watching a film with violence in it you're getting involved in the film, but when you see something that's hundreds of miles away it's upsetting to watch but at the end of the day you can't get emotional about it.

She was alone in her opinion:

> *I disagree with that — when it's fictional it's not happening. With this you think 'shit, that's really happening', no matter where they are in the world.*
>
> *If it's a film you could watch it but because it's real you can't.*

Description of violence is not of violence

We followed the Sarajevo clip by a scene from *Panorama* on killings in Rwanda. In the clip youngsters have been arrested for killing members of an opposing tribe, and are interviewed by the *Panorama* team. The youngsters describe the killings, show remorse, and claim that they were forced to commit the crimes. The accounts moved the respondents, but did they regard reported events as violence? At first it seemed that young men talking about how they had killed people might be defined as violence:

> *Yes, people being forced to kill someone they knew.*

But such a conclusion was not sustained, and as the discussion progressed the feeling changed:

> *It's more about violence, it's not actually violence.*

This response was general to all groups, and reinforces the point that to define something as violent one must see the violence in action. Nor would this group have wished to see real violence of a serious nature:

> *To see violence is frightening — one person hurting another. To hear violence or to hear about violence doesn't have the same impact.*
>
> *I wouldn't mind seeing the kid lying there [after a landmine explosion] but I don't want to see it actually happen.*

Action on screen seems to have a 'present moment' rather than a 'past moment' feel to it. A real injury which is 'in the past' has an entirely different impact to a fictional injury that takes place as the viewer watches.

Violence & nature

The reaction of these women to the documentary on bear-baiting was remarkably similar to the reactions of the 'hard' young men. It was violent because one saw the bear attacked, and it was violent in a way that a fight in the wild would not have been. The injuries were contrived – they followed from the actions of humans and not the actions of the animals themselves. In discussing animals in the wild, someone observed:

> *That's nature isn't it, that's what goes on, there is not a lot you can do about that but when you're forcing it into this situation where you're disadvantaging the bear that's not nature.*

It was agreed that because the bear was deliberately disadvantaged it was an unfair contest, and that made it more violent. We put it to them that had the bear not had its teeth removed and claws drawn then they would, 'certainly have seen a lot more blood', and asked if the scene would then have been more or less violent. They agreed that it would:

> *It would have been more violent but not as distressing.*
> *It wouldn't have altered how cruel it is but it would have been more violent.*

It seems that emotion does enter into a definition of violence – it was unfair, and the unfairness enhanced the cruelty, which then added to the sense of violence – but nevertheless the real criterion for the sequence's violence was not subjective but objective: blood. In other words, to have seen more blood would have been to see more violence, because one would have seen more action.

Atmospheric violence

We used a clip from *Schindler's List* to see if emotion and building up tension might be seen as violence. The part chosen was the shower scene in Auschwitz, where the women inmates are taken to the shower, believing they are to be gassed. In the film the tension builds, and the faces of the women increasingly register fear, until the tension is broken when water and not gas comes out of the shower heads. It was not seen as violent:

> *No, not violent. Evil, nasty and cruel maybe, but not violent.*

We introduced the clip from *Schindler's List* to only one other group as it was clearly not categorised as violence. The point of the exercise was to see if the threat of violence, and the belief that death was about to happen – 'I thought they were going to be gassed' – could be defined as violent in the way that, in special circumstances, verbal abuse could be violent. Also, we noticed that while something being 'cruel' does not make it violent, if an act considered violent is accompanied by cruelty, then often it will be seen as violent with a big V, rather than with a little v.

Comic violence

As a final exercise with this group we showed a clip from the comedy programme *Bottom*, where one character has his head repeatedly smashed on the counter of a bar and spits out teeth in almost cartoon fashion. There is blood, but not much. No-one considered this scene violent at all – the comic aspect to the proceedings de-focused the violence:

> *People know that that's not actually happening.*
> *They over-exaggerate everything.*

In other words, this is neither authentic violence nor depicted violence. All the members of this group had seen *Pulp Fiction*, and although the violence there is depicted violence, the scene where Marvin in the back of the car has his face shot away was not classed as violent at all:

> *Not violent, just a bit sick.*

And when we asked them to reconsider their decision that it was not violent, mentioning 'There's a lot of blood isn't there?', one respondent replied:

> *Oh yes, but I think it's a mickey-take of every form of gangster violence that you can imagine.*

She recognised the rules by which the violence was being played, and felt that to parody cinema violence – and a particular form, gangster violence – was to remove its seriousness as violence.

4

Policing Violence

The sample included a group of working policemen. Although the possibility of violence was ever-present in their work, it was only one aspect of it. Like most jobs it had its routine, even boring, element. In discussing *The Bill*, one of them said:

The problem with that is that it's five weeks' work in half an hour. You can go out for eight hours and see nothing but they get the whole thing into half an hour or an hour. The procedures are excellent and the research is fantastic.

Someone else added:

Nobody would watch it if it was real. If it was 100 per cent real it would be the most boring programme ever put out on TV.

And someone else said:

PC Penrose is probably more true to life.

On the whole they did not relish police programmes. Even though most were considered 'unreal', to watch them was a busman's holiday:

I think when you've been at work all day the last thing you want to do is go home and see something like that.

Inspector Morse was enjoyed, but then Morse falls more into the genre of Whodunnit than police fiction.

Experience of violence

When asked what was the 'worst violence you have come across in your job', they singled out the poll tax riots:

Probably the poll tax riots – that was violence on a large scale.

Given the violence that they later described, this was surprising, and our surprise may have showed in our question:

[Prompt] Was there much blood about?

Not really, it was the potential violence. People's attitudes towards you as well. It was pure hatred – from an early stage that day as well.

At times we were in control but at other times we weren't and what was going on that day was quite frightening. The scale of what was happening was quite harrowing.

It was a funny sort of atmosphere really. The scale of the whole thing and the noise that was going on, it had a strange feel about it. I wouldn't like to go through that again.

The experience of real violence sheds some light on the definition of screen violence. These policemen clearly felt that hatred was a factor in creating a violent atmosphere. In the same way, in *Ladybird, Ladybird*, the man's anger increased the feeling of violence.

These men experienced fear during the Poll Tax Riots. This helps us to understand how acts on screen appear violent. Although they had the collective support of their colleagues, these policemen were not accustomed to the type of events, and the type of violence, that occurred. It was a different to the type of violence they were used to, and at times they felt powerless to control the flow of events. The novelty gave rise to surprise, and the powerlessness gave rise to fear. We have seen already that novel violence is more likely to be defined as violent than familiar violence, and that the victim's powerlessness and fear are key factors in defining violence.

The Poll Tax riot, which clearly made a lasting impression on these policemen, was collective, public violence, but we wanted to know their reactions to the personal violence that was more usual in their working life. One officer said:

To be honest, in my job you're more likely to go to an address after it's happened.

We asked what was his reaction the first time he had had to 'go to an address':

It's difficult to explain, but you end up laughing about it – the smell of bleach where they've tried to clean the blood off the walls, things like that. You don't take it seriously.

The statement, 'You don't take it seriously', shows how humour de-focuses the violence, which becomes no more than a foible of human nature. We wanted to press the point about his reaction to the sight of so much blood that bleach was needed to remove it: 'I just wondered if you weren't shocked the first time and then you became accustomed to it?'

> *I don't know whether you become accustomed to it or whether it just becomes part of what you do.*

A colleague explained further:

> *It's all you ever expected. When you first start out you expect it and when you first see it you're normally with people with more experience so you expect it straight away. You think about it afterwards and then you just get on with it.*

Getting to used to violence

What they are saying is that one can get accustomed to the sight of damage caused by violence so that it is no longer disturbing. That is to be expected, and it supports the argument advanced earlier: watching screen violence may accustom the individual to screen violence, and witnessing real life violence accustoms the individual to that type of violence, but there is no necessary connection between the two.

We went on to discuss different types of violence. We asked, 'Is some violence more upsetting than others or is it all the same?'

> *There are different grades. If you go to a Scottish club where all the blokes are drunk and they've slashed each other you're not going to be as upset as if an old lady has been cut up by a burglar. You grade it in your own mind. If some drug dealer has been beaten up and had his jewellery nicked it's not going to worry you as much as an old lady who's been kicked around the flat and had her pension taken.*
>
> *[Prompt] Do you ever get very upset or do you not get involved?*
>
> *I think you have to step away from it. I know people who do get very involved with old ladies who've been beaten up, they go round and see them on a weekly basis, which is okay but you can't do it for everybody.*

Premeditated violence to me is shocking. Somebody who's been kneecapped with a hatchet or somebody who has systematically tortured someone is shocking. A lot of people do things on the spur of the moment — they can do something in a rage, in drink, but when you go out and do something premeditated that's worse.

You tend to find nine times out of ten that the victim of the crime has asked for it and you tend to find that the type of people they become involved with are criminals. It's criminals versus criminals. We tend to turn round and say, perhaps they deserved it. Most victims of violence are violent people.

[Prompt] That lessens the impact does it?

Yes, it's an everyday occurrence. In a pub fight the guy who gets a chair across his head is likely to have been putting a chair across somebody else's head to start with. It's rare, thankfully, that you get a completely innocent person being attacked for no reason.

We asked: 'You obviously expect violence in your job, but attending a scene like that [a bad traffic accident], did it shock you'?

Yes I'll never forget it — the smell. I wouldn't say I couldn't go and do it again though.

One of his colleagues picked up the theme:

I don't think it's always the nastiest ones that stay in your mind. Sometimes where say someone is trapped and you can't get them out but you strike up a conversation with them. You stay with them until the fire brigade gets there. That can be quite difficult at times.

[Prompt] Was that more upsetting than the crimes of violence that you go to?

It's difficult to say because you're trying to generalise and every occasion is different. Every situation you go to can surprise you. For instance, we went to a stabbing a few weeks ago where the bloke had been stabbed through the chest with a screwdriver and pinned to the floor and it wasn't upsetting until we realised that an eight year old had witnessed it and was hiding in a room upstairs. So each one is different for different reasons.

Constructing violence & judging the person

Here the same principles are at work in defining real life violence as operate in defining screen violence. If the victim is innocent, it is more upsetting than if he is not. In certain situations they can take the violence in their stride, the equivalent in real life of screen violence with a little v. Similarly, cruelty increases the sense of violence in real life, as on the screen. And again, we see how scenes of violence can unfold in real life, as on the screen. The pinning to the floor by a screwdriver through the chest was shocking, but it became more shocking as the scene unfolded to reveal a child hiding in an upstairs room. The parallel is plain if we go back to comments made about the two young children looking on in *Ladybird, Ladybird*. Although not agreeing that it made the scene more violent, the respondents undoubtedly thought their presence increased the impact of the violence.

Unrealistic action

Having established how these policeman defined their experience of violence in real life, we proceeded, as with all the groups, to show them the clips of screen violence. We began with the clip from *Thief Takers*. The following is the transcript of their comments, and questions from the moderator. At first, one or two said:

> *I think that would qualify as violent.*

> *It's extremely violent.*

We were somewhat surprised by such definitions, but it soon began to appear that what they meant was that this was violence with a little v, and the comment that 'it's extremely violent' meant that it contained a lot of little v. It was not big V, as the following judgements show.

> *It was violent but it was so unrealistic it would almost be cartoon like*

> *If you wanted to make that really violent then you would have a more realistic situation where the one with the machine gun would have shot all the rest. That would have been real violence.*

He is probably right. Had the Russian gangster shot every one, then, instead of choreographed mayhem, we would have had brutal carnage. The clip was seen as too unreal to be considered serious violence. A professional eye was cast over the scene:

> *It's very shallow — instead of a few weeks of activity being condensed down, that's a whole career and more.*

In other words, it is too far-fetched to be taken seriously. But there were other observations:

> It's not violence though is it? To me a gun is not violent. When you talk to me about violence it's physical violence, kicking and punching.
>
> It's not intimate violence, they're just pointing something and you see somebody fall back.
>
> It's not really portraying what a gun can do to someone anyway. It's verging on the comical. They would have been completely obliterated by a machine gun.

This violence was unrealistic violence, and therefore did not count as real violence. It was not only that the damage inflicted by the gun was unrealistic. The whole scene was difficult to accept as an accurate picture of police activity. If a scene is not 'true to life', even if the violence in it is 'realistic', it will not add up to a definition of big V.

The discussion about *Thief Takers* showed that for something to be considered violent, the violence must be 'intimate', where intimate means direct physical contact – 'kicking and punching'.

We next showed the group the cinema version of *Deep Cover* where the informer is beaten with a pool cue.

> It's violent, but I've seen the film and it's good.
>
> I think the shock on the people's face makes it violent.
>
> And the spray of blood
>
> They had the sound – everyone here has probably heard something similar. That for me is the thing that makes it more real. Obviously he hasn't been hit but he may well have been because it was well done.
>
> Yes, great sound effects.
>
> It was still self-edited. You never actually saw the cue hitting the guy across the face.

These policeman were asked: 'Have you ever seen that type of beating?'

> I've seen a pub fight but not one with everybody standing around.
>
> It's the pace of the thing. When you're in a pub fight it's over in seconds, but that's a voyeur's side to it, holding someone down.
>
> It's a realistic portrayal of violence of that type, but we wouldn't see that because the first time you saw someone hitting someone else you'd get to them.

Although it was considered violent, it was also considered a good film, especially when compared with *Thief Takers*. This group appreciated the realistic violence, and what it real was the sound. Although these policeman said, 'Everyone here has probably heard something similar', none of them had witnessed such a prolonged beating. Even to a group with experience of violence, the scene was still only an imagined portrayal. Drawing on first-hand experience, the policemen considered that such a beating would result in more blood – 'be lots of claret'. This group, who were well placed to pronounce on realism, criticised the 'pace of violence', saying that real violence is often 'over in seconds', and that this scene had a 'voyeur's side to it'.

Voyeurism violence

Voyeurism is built into the scene by the helplessness of the victom on the pool table, and by making the viewers witness the violence both through their own eyes, and also vicariously, through the eyes of the onlookers. All 'depicted' screen violence is voyeuristic. The viewer is invited to look closely, and observe the detail of injury. To achieve this, the action is often slowed down, and this is so even where actual slow motion techniques are not employed. As one of the respondents said:

> *It's the pace of the thing... in a pub fight it's over in seconds.*

To have something over in seconds is to miss the 'moment of injury'. Only by focusing the camera on the point of the action and removing the clutter of other movements can violence be made slow enough to be fully taken in. It is not 'real', but it is 'realistic' in a cinematic sense. The sound also helped to carry the violence into the mind, and this is interesting. If you take the comment that it was the sound that made it violent, together with the comment, 'You never actually saw the cue hitting the guy', this adds up to a modification of the rule that you have to show the action to make it violent.

In Hitchcock's shower scene in *Psycho*, one does not see the knife enter the body, and the scene is not seen as violent with a big V. Yet in *Deep Cover* we have the reverse: as with Hitchcock, we do not see the blows being struck, and yet the scene is defined as violent. As with Hitchcock there is blood, which this group considered violent, and we hear the blows plus the screams of pain. No-one in any of the other groups noticed that the blows to the face were never actually seen, but they all had a strong impression of having seen them. If viewers think they have seen the actual impact of a violent blow – an arm severed, a bullet entering a body – then they will classify the scene as violent. If viewers have the impression that they have seen a violent act, they react in the same way as when they have seen a violent act. The suggestion of violence works as violence so long as the viewer is 'fooled'.

Noise & mood as violence

We asked the group to edit the clip to extend the discussion of what made it violent. The suggestions were:

> *Try and take the noise out.*
> *His pain, take that away, the screaming.*
> *It's the impact sound for me.*
> *Just leave one blow in, the initial one.*

No-one asked for the blood to be edited, even though in the initial discussion 'the spray of blood' was mentioned as contributing to the scene being defined as violent. After editing, mainly by altering the sound, the clip was judged again:

> *That doesn't appear as violent – the noise is less.*

It was the noise that gave the impression of ferocity – the sheer unleashing of force through sound. The next edit was to remove the shots of those watching the beating. In the initial discussion, showing the faces, and the looks of revulsion they displayed, was thought to have heightened the violence. After the edit, opinions were reversed:

> *It's still violent.*
> *It's more intense.*
> *[Prompt] So what you're saying is that by taking out the faces of the people looking on, we have actually concentrated more on the beatings and the action?*
> *Yes. It's a severe beating but the fact that you've got the faces, it gives your brain a bit of a chance to recover. It's a quite cleverly shot film.*

When pressed to say what he meant by 'cleverly shot', he replied:

> *It's difficult to say because I think it's an excellent film. I think the whole film expresses the mood very well and it's quite scary and realistic.*

It will be remembered that when the 'hard' young men edited this scene they took out the onlookers to make the violence more strong.

Mood is important and we shall come back to it, but for the moment what we can say is that violence appears stronger if the viewer is allowed no diversion. Focusing continuously on the violence creates a feeling that it is actually happening.

Now let us return to the question of 'mood'. Editing out the surrounding action focused the viewer's attention, and made the violence more 'intense'. This doesn't mean that the revulsion on the faces of the gang members did not add to the feeling of violence. It did. As one of the policemen said:

> *They were presumably in with this guy who was whacking him, and even they're shocked. If they're frightened by it and they're in the firm it frightens me.*
>
> *[Prompt] Does real heavy violence have to involve some kind of fear?*
>
> *Yes, I would say so.*
>
> *If you're not fearful you're not frightened of violence.*
>
> *Your question about the fear. If you have a guy in handcuffs who's taking a beating and he can't react to it then that's fearful, but if they can react to it and do something back then the fear aspect drains away. If you've got an equal situation then the stronger one is going to win.*
>
> *[Prompt] Does that make it less violent?*
>
> *No it doesn't make it less violent.*
>
> *Part of the way it makes it violent is the fact that this man is surrounded by people who could help him but won't. They could all do something. We don't know what he's done to deserve the beating.*

Enjoyment of punishment

We asked, 'Does the status of the victim make a difference?'

> *Yes. If you were to relate it to another film – I think it was Goodfellas where the waiter got shot – that is violence because the guy had done nothing, he was just wandering around.*

This point was picked up, since one of the participants had mentioned earlier that if he did not like the victim, he positively enjoyed any violence inflicted. We asked:

[Prompt] Does it mean that you can actually enjoy the violence?

Yes, if someone deserves it.

Yes, the other night Redemption was on and I would quite happily have seen the bad guy beaten to death with a baseball bat because he deserved everything he got.

That's why you don't often see a woman or a child being beaten on television because most people won't accept that, whereas if it's a guy who's been involved in something then it's fair game.

Most people would have difficulty in accepting images of women and children being beaten, but the point of these comments – as we have seen with earlier groups – is that 'justice' enters the frame when considering violence. Violence with 'justice' on its side can be more freely enjoyed:

I would have quite happily seen the bad guy beaten to death with a baseball bat.

The prohibition of violence against women and children is a moral point: those who are not equipped to stand up to physical force are deserve protection more than those who are suitably equipped. Watching violence against the weak cannot be pleasurable, since to find it enjoyable would be to subvert one's moral values. To enjoy violence one must have values that allow you to enjoy it. The policeman, for example, was able to enjoy the 'bad guy' being beaten because he 'deserved everything he got'.

Reactions of the police group to domestic violence followed a similar pattern. We first showed the scene from *Brookside* and asked: 'Was that violent?'

It's not acceptable is it? – not on television.

They didn't have to show the violence did they?

We asked the group if they wished to edit the material, but that brought problems.

It was the sound again.

I would turn that off.

I think you could see it coming.

You know she's going to get smacked — that's what makes it violent.

To be honest with you it's the time that it is shown. That's way beyond what should be shown.

[Prompt] If it went out at 10 o'clock at night, would you still hold it to be violent?

It's violent, but you wouldn't criticise it.

In coming to the defence of *Brookside*, someone added:

I find Brookside out of all the Soaps quite enjoyable.

This comment carried the discussion forward:

I think Brookside *shows scenes that you don't really want to watch but they are realistic. Wife beating happens. The way it was portrayed on that programme was good — it was upsetting because of the material but it was portrayed in a light where you didn't actually see blows being made.*

Following this observation, someone said:

If you take the sound of her screaming out then what have you got?

You couldn't because it wouldn't make it realistic.

It's the build up which leads to it, not the actual act.

[Prompt] Can you have a violent atmosphere?

Of course you can. If you watch old films you can have an extremely violent atmosphere without actually seeing any violence.

[Prompt] Would you class it as violence even if you don't see it?

No, it's an atmosphere.

You don't need violence to enjoy the fear.

'Enjoying the fear' did not refer to *Brookside*, but to violent atmospheres in general. Hitchcock was mentioned in this context:

I would have far more nightmares from Hitchcock than I would from that but I'd find that more unacceptable than Hitchcock.

A few points here. The noise once more created the violence. In fact, the noise 'stood in' for the violence. They considered that this scene could not be edited without detracting from the point being made, namely the nastiness of domestic violence. Taken literally, the scene is not very violent: what makes it violent is the subject matter. With domestic violence, values and moral judgements come surging to the fore. When it is held to be wrong, even 'weak' violence becomes 'strong'. This classically illustrates the point: what is morally disturbing is more violent.

Values, therefore, can increase the chance of a scene being defined as violent. Objections to *Brookside* had less to do with the level, than with the type, of violence shown. Some of these objections spring from discomfort in confronting such behaviour. As one of the policeman said: 'I would turn it off'.

Producer violence

Before they were able to use 'depicted violence', or 'researched violence', film makers had to create frightening violence by atmosphere alone. What has occurred since, and what was recognised by this group, is that violence has been producer-driven, with each new breakthrough in technique triggering new definitions of what is 'violent'. Other violence, not corresponding with depicted or researched violence, is classified as non-violent. Atmospheric violence is no longer read as violence unless accompanied by depicted violence. A violent atmosphere simply assists the impact of the violence, and does not constitute violence in itself.

Upsetting violence

Given that we expected the police group to have had occupational contact with domestic violence, we wanted to relate their experiences to the scenes in *Ladybird, Ladybird*.

We began by saying: 'You've said that attending car accidents is upsetting. What is the most upsetting type of violence that you go to – you mentioned old age pensioners. Do you see serious domestic violence?'

There was some hesitation in replying, and, before the first person spoke, eye contact was made with one or two other officers which, along with expressions made, clearly signalled that he was looking for agreement that he should speak openly about such experiences. After all we were 'outsiders' to the policemen's world.

Understandably, the policemen were cautious of giving accounts of their experience which, to the outsider, might appear unsympathetic to the victims of domestic violence:

> *To be honest they're living how you could never imagine you would live — the poor, downtrodden way of life that they live. You don't feel sorry for them because you know next week he's going to be back in the house and doing it again. You feel sorry for the children. It's a sad fact of life. You take the bloke away and the wife doesn't want to make a statement. You become cold towards it. They live lives that you can't appreciate anyone could live.*
>
> *[Prompt] Does it lessen the violence then?*
>
> *Of course it does because you go to a domestic violence incident and the wife says she wants to prosecute and you spend all your time doing all the paperwork and you go back and the wife says she's changed her mind and doesn't want him prosecuted. And you do it again and again, so it hardens you to it.*
>
> *[Prompt] So the fourth time you've been back you don't classify it as violence?*
>
> *You do, but it affects the way you perceive it and want to pursue it.*
>
> *I find it more upsetting going to see an old lady who has lost all her savings.*

These policemen were toughened by their job, but they were far from uncaring about the 'human condition'. They appeared to have a strong sense of social justice, and a warmth for the victims of other people's callousness. But after repeated visits to the same house, the emotive impact of domestic violence was spent — 'You become cold towards it'.

This coldness was not brutal or uncaring. It was not that the victim was responsible for her injuries. But her unwillingness to avail herself of legal protection meant, at the very least, that it was difficult to take the victim's 'outrage' seriously — and, one might argue, the violence itself seriously — although in an objective sense they recognised that serious violence had taken place. Another member of the group said:

> *If you did a survey amongst police about who were the most despised people it would be those who rob old people, apart from the obvious*

ones like paedophiles. What people don't recognise is that these old ladies usually die six months later.

[Prompt] So, if there was a gang in a film who had done that to old ladies and then been caught and beaten up, would you see that as less violent than if the gang had done nothing?

You'd enjoy the violence.

I think generally if you asked people they wouldn't mind the level of violence been taken quite high in cases like that.

Most drama involves a moral tale, and it is difficult to leave behind the moral judgements of the 'outside' world when viewing drama. In the case of these policeman, the way they graded the social seriousness of an offence – as opposed to its legal seriousness – was carried over to their judgement of violence on screen. The seriousness of domestic violence itself was never underestimated by these policemen, but there was less sympathy for the victims if they refused to avail themselves of legal protection, which then coloured their response to the violence.

Authentic violence

Much of what this group said about their professional experience of domestic violence is echoed in their reactions to *Ladybird, Ladybird*. We set out to discover if their values influenced their definition and acceptance of violence:

That's realistic – it's horrible, but it's realistic.

She's defenceless. You can see what's going to happen.

I must admit I was relieved to see him smacking the beer can on the carpet rather than in her face.

I thought he did hit her actually.

That is violence – anybody would find that violent.

It's also the language [cunt].

That is unacceptable to anybody I know. It's the way he said it as well.

If you take the children away it's still unacceptable.

Nothing you could do to that would alter it. Unless you cut it where he's boiling up on the sofa. I think you're wasting your time.

That's an excellent portrayal of domestic violence — that's how severe it gets.

Unless you chop the whole scene — just see him boiling up and then storming out and then you see her face, that would probably be the only way to make it acceptable. But even that would be upsetting.

It's so sudden — she hasn't done anything to upset him except be late.

In real life the wife does quite often wind up the husband to get him to that level of violence.

[Prompt] If she had been having a go at him again and again and he turned around and hit her would that be more acceptable?

The whole point is that that is a man hitting a woman as hard as he can — that is domestic violence.

[Prompt] But if she had been provoking him, would it seem less violent when he does actually hit her?

I think that level of violence is unacceptable whatever you preamble it with.

As one of the policemen said: 'That is violence — anybody would find that violent'. Not only was this violence — authentic violence located in the world of each viewer — but it collected together practically all the components discussed so far that constitute a definition of violence. It involved close contact (punching and kicking); a helpless victim; pain; fear; repetitive blows; injury continuing long past establishing a point; unequal distribution of power; violence out of proportion to the offence committed; language as assault. It was overlaid with secondary violence by the presence of the children, who stood helplessly by as they saw one parent damage another.

This violence is very powerful, and there is a limit to how much the viewer can accept. As one of the respondents said: 'I must admit I was relieved to see him smacking the beer can on the carpet rather than in her face'.

Sensitivity & values

The policemen mentioned a loss of sympathy for victims who repeatedly failed to avail themselves of help. They said that the victim would sometimes come to the station and refuse to press charges, and sometimes express fondness for their violent partner.

In the case of *Ladybird, Ladybird* the policeman were unequivocal. They did not in any way allow such considerations to affect their definition of domestic violence: '...she hasn't done anything to upset him except be late'. Even if she had, there could be no excuse as far as they were concerned for this level of violence.

Although the violence in *Ladybird, Ladybird* is in one sense not as severe as that in *Deep Cover* – where, shown in gory detail, the victim is severely beaten – the policemen saw it as more violent. They were relieved that a beer can was smashed on the floor beside the woman's head, and not on her head.

Before leaving *Ladybird, Ladybird* it is worth noting that, disturbing though the scene was to these policemen, they did not believe it was possible to edit the clip – it came as a package. To make cuts that would lower the violence would be wrong, since to do so would detract from the reality of domestic violence as they knew it to be. In this case, the viewer and the producer, Ken Loach, were in agreement over the intention of the film. Later, however, we shall see that the older women in our sample did want cuts to be made.

Editing impact

We have termed the domestic violence of *Ladybird, Ladybird* 'authentic violence'. It occurs in the real world inhabited by the viewer. From this representational, but authentic, violence, we moved on to show real violence, presenting the scene where the young Italian man is attacked for stealing a teddy-bear left to commemorate Diana, Princess of Wales.

We first showed the rushes and the stumbling, barely articulate, drunken Scotsman who throws the punch to the head of the Italian. They found the scene funny:

I've been attacked by him and his relatives a few times.

They recognised the type of drunk only too well, and suggested he had probably just come from the court himself. The immediate comment was: 'You felt that didn't you?'. Asked if it was violent.

Yes, but you could see it coming.

I didn't think it was particularly violent. I thought the assailant was quite a laughable character.

A lot of people felt that he deserved to get punched because of the public feeling at the time.

We then showed the version broadcast by Sky News. One respondent considered it looked 'less violent' because 'there was no build up'. Most thought otherwise:

I thought it more violent myself because you didn't see the character — it was more sudden, before you could see it coming.

If I was going to maximise the effect that is how I'd put it out. You dramatise it. It gave the impression that every single member of the British public wanted to beat this man to death because of what he did.

The edited version made the blow look as if it had been delivered by an outraged citizen, representing the viewers themselves. We asked if the second blow appeared more violent:

It was a good punch. I think it was a clever bit of evidence. Rather than editing the violence to lower the effect, that heightened it really.

That's the way I'd put it out if I wanted to get the viewers because it did look better.

One or two comments are worth making here. To begin with, none of these officers saw the scenes, especially the first one, as in the least threatening. To them it was all manageable violence, and not likely to get out of control. Had these officers been at the scene then no violence would have been necessary even to effect an arrest. Although not exactly harmless, as the Italian found to his cost, the drunk was not capable of inflicting much harm:

You'd only have to give him the slightest push and he'd fall over.

In the first shot, these men had sympathy for neither the assailant nor the victim. Their comments demonstrate that their attitude to violence is modified when the violence has some moral authority: in this case, the Italian got his 'due desserts' for desecrating a shrine. The editing 'sharpened' the blow, and therefore increased the impression of hurt. At the same time it reduced the moral equivocation of the violence by excluding the drunk as a person. In the first clip he hardly looked the part of an avenging angel. In the second clip he isn't there, and the punch becomes the punch of justice. In this case, the less you see of the scene, the greater the impression of violence. The more you see of the scene, the less the impact of violence.

Empathy with the victim

Given that the policeman were accustomed to witnessing the results of both deliberate and accidental violence, we were especially interested in their responses to the Reuters footage of the carnage following the bombing of Tulsa. They did not, as with everyone else this was shown to, consider that in witnessing the destruction they were witnessing violence. It was the aftermath of violence. In the course of the discussion one of the officers mentioned the scene shown on British television a few years ago, shot from an army helicopter, of two soldiers in plain clothes who had been captured by the IRA after inadvertently losing direction and driving their car into an area where an IRA funeral was taking place:

> *They [television] showed the violence of the IRA shooting of the two soldiers.*

The pictures were shot from a distance by a helicopter, but the unfolding of events, the struggle that took place, and the final dispatch of the soldiers was clearly seen.

> *You tended to think that was violence because you could imagine what it was like to be that person. You could feel the fear they were experiencing and you could put yourself in their shoes.*

> *[Prompt] If we hadn't had the film of the action itself and we'd just seen the bodies of the soldiers afterwards, would that have been as violent?*

> *That's just dead bodies isn't it?.*

> *I think the whole point was that you felt for them — you felt it could have been you.*

The fact that they could put themselves in the place of the soldiers may be a response special to this group. Even if they haven't themselves been in life-threatening situations, they know that they could, like the soldiers, find themselves in such situations. All the same, they classified the scene as violent because it involved witnessing violent acts, and not out of special sympathy with the soldiers.

The group returned to discuss the Tulsa clip and the picture of the near-decapitated woman:

> I think whoever said it was shocking rather than violent was right. The scene to me with the pool cue is more violent than that. That's the aftermath.

The shots were horrifying, and evoked pity, but they were not classified as violence.

Experience of death

Most groups shown the Reuters footage showed signs of being upset while watching it. Not the policemen. Calling the scene 'shocking and upsetting', but adding, 'it's not violent', the strongest image picked out was 'the woman's face'. Someone said:

> That's similar to some road traffic accidents to be honest.
>
> I didn't see any of you flinch when looking at that.
>
> Well, we've all seen dead bodies.
>
> I think over the years seeing all the things I've seen, it's taken the edge off footage like that
>
> The thing is that one of the first things you do in our job is go to the morgue. I think that's quite a good technique to use.
>
> [Prompt] What is your position on the argument that if we keep watching stuff like that, when we do see it in real life it becomes less shocking?
>
> It's a totally different thing to see in real life.
>
> The thing that comes home when you're in a real life situation is the smell, the sound that's going on around you.

Later in the discussion:

> Life has become more censored. We don't actually come across death in the normal course of events. When a relative dies we have very little contact with them. Years ago you would go into the room with them – now most of the public aren't aware of death.

Less 'censorship' of screen violence means that we see more images of death and dying. Increased 'censorship' of death in real life means that we have less exposure to the actual experience of death. As we have seen, vicarious experience of injury and death on screen is not the same as first-hand experience.

5

Controlling fear, controlling violence

Our next group was recruited on the basis that they were afraid of crime, although they had not been the victims of crime. They were all women, aged between 25 and 40. We wanted to include a group with a high degree of fear of crime to see if their definitions of screen violence differed from those of others in our sample.

Nervousness & violence

Crime against the person is not common. We heard from the police group that, 'most victims of violence are violent people'. Yet fear of violence is strong in many people who live far from sites of violence.

First we discussed what programmes this group found violent. Then we asked: 'How about violence in real life – do you worry about muggings and things like that?' They were totally honest:

> *Yes, even parking my car here tonight I was worried about where I was going to park. You feel quite vulnerable.*

> *Even in the day when I stop at lights I always put the button down because I've always got my bag on the passenger seat – or somebody getting in the car.*

> *Even in the day when I'm driving on my own I put my handbag handle through the seat belt. It's not just at night.*

We asked, 'Do you feel nervous if you're at home on your own?' They did. One woman, however, said no: 'Not at home, but I've got dogs'. Others, with or without dogs, were nervous:

I'm a bit worried if the doorbell rings and I'm at home on my own.

I don't open the door at all at night.

[Prompt] Are there any other precautions you take or is it mainly outside the house that you feel vulnerable?

I always make sure everything is locked up and if I hear a noise it worries me.

We've got lights all round the house so if anyone comes near they all come on.

We had a privet hedge round the garden when we moved in and we had a fence put round so anyone would have to jump over it rather than just go through the hedge.

[Prompt] Do you keep any weapons in the house?

We have a cricket bat in case any one of us hears anything.

We've got a baseball bat.

We've got a truncheon.

We've got a panic button by our bed and by our front door.

They were asked: 'When you were younger were you equally nervous?' They claimed not to have been. Although their nervousness appeared to have developed with age, their given reasons for feeling apprehensive had nothing to do with age:

I suppose it's television — the news.

And Crimewatch.

Even picking up the local paper and seeing people talking about what happened to them.

The imagination & fear of the real

Their anxieties stemmed from the fear that what had happened to others might happen to them: a reasonable enough fear. We wanted to check: 'Have any of you had any unfortunate experiences yourself?' None had, but:

My daughter [aged 15] gets driven and fetched everywhere. She has a panic alarm in her pocket and I make my son [aged 13] take it as well when he's going out. He's been stopped by other boys.

[Prompt] Do you worry at all if your partner is late home?

I do because my husband is a bank manager and they have been warned about kidnappings and things like that. So we're particularly aware of it and if he's late home I worry.

We began, as we always did, with *Thief Takers*. Their responses were different from other groups. All agreed that the scene was violent, but not especially violent:

Yes, I would watch it, but I would still think of it as violent.

I don't particularly mind all the shooting — it's the bits in slow motion I don't want to see and I don't think it's necessary. I know it's all for effect.

I don't like to see head-butting — I'd rather see the shooting than that.

We asked if the head-butting was more violent than the shooting:

Yes it was for me.

Anybody can head-butt, but not many people have got guns'.

This group found it difficult to distance themselves from what they saw on the screen. For example, in discussing *Deep Cover* and comparing it with the violence in *Thief Takers*, one women said that *Deep Cover* was 'more realistic' because:

Somebody wouldn't come into a restaurant with all those guns, but perhaps somebody would attack you with a baseball bat.

This group did want to make cuts in *Thief Takers*. There was general agreement that the restaurant scene would be made less violent if it was cut 'Where the first man got shot and the bullet went straight though his back'. They wanted to edit the site of the violence — the bullet entering the back — and remove the slow motion sequence which, it had already been agreed, heightened the violence. They also wanted the noise accompanying the head-butt to be lowered. These cuts were effected and it was held to be less violent by some, but, given that it was not considered particularly violent in the first place, the edits were not considered especially effective. For the first time slow motion was mentioned as increasing violence.

Feelings of involvement

The violence of *Deep Cover* was held to be 'much worse' than the violence in *Thief Takers*. We asked what made it worse.

It was repetitive.

The sound effects definitely made a difference — you could almost feel it.

These responses have been heard before, but what is different is the personalising of the violence.

It made me cringe.

I think perhaps the bystanders watching made it violent as well — the fact that it was obviously disturbing to them — you could see they were frightened.

[Prompt] Did that make you become more involved?

She said, 'Yes', but added:

You were one of the bystanders.

They did not consider that this film could be cut:

I just wouldn't go to watch that.

No, I wouldn't go. I think it would be difficult to cut bits from that.

It was not difficult to cut; others did, and, indeed, Carlton had cut it. Having no taste for violence, the clip seemed to them so preoccupied with violence that there was no point in cutting it. Nevertheless we showed them the version edited by Carlton Television:

There is just less of it — it was just as violent.

[Prompt] Do you know what was taken out?

The bit where he was on the table and the spray of blood.

We asked if the broadcast version was more acceptable:

There is no necessity for the first version.

You still get the idea of what's happening.

It was just as disturbing, but without some of the graphics.

It did not go on for so long.

The reduction in the length of the scene was appreciated:

On the second one by the time you start to think 'that's awful', it's over.

Carlton's version is considerably milder than the cinema version. But to this group 'it was just as violent' because the same basic message was there — that the world is a violent place. Some of this group did find the second version more acceptable, but one felt that here the question being addressed was one of taste and decency, and not violence as such – 'There is no necessity for the first version'.

Emotional response to violence

The way this group defined violence differed from other groups. They were less analytical in their approach, and more emotional. More than other respondents, they tended to discuss the violence in terms of what effect it had upon them: they centred on themselves rather than on the material.

We showed the group the battle scene from *Culloden*, shot in black and white. They considered it 'quite' violent. One respondent said:

> *I think black and white makes a difference. One of the reasons why I found it not quite so harrowing as it could have been was because it was shot in black and white.*

This led her to discuss *Schindler's List*, also in black and white.

> *You saw the blood but it wasn't red. There was one particular scene where there was a girl kneeling on the floor and he just shot her through the back of the head and you saw black blood coming out of the front of her head and I'm sure it was as graphic as it could be, but because it was in black and white it wasn't so harrowing.*

Culloden led to a discussion of historical drama:

> *It's not gratuitous violence is it – it actually happened.*

> *I think we're still disturbed by a film like that because it was factual rather than make-believe.*

But then came the key statement:

> *It makes you disgusted, but not frightened. It's not threatening because it happened so long ago.*

Discussions with this group often came round to what the violence meant to them and what it did to them – it frightened them. Violence in the past did not frighten them, because it was not something that might happen in their own lives.

Feeling safe affecting response

Given that *Ladybird, Ladybird* is authentic violence, one might expect that it would be defined as massively violent and found to be deeply upsetting by this group. This was not so. It was seen as violent and it was held to be upsetting, but not to the extent that we expected. For this showing of the film we decided to split the group into two, and to have one group see the version as transmitted, and the second group view an edited version in which the sound of the blows had been lowered. Both groups were then reconvened to watch the original broadcast version together. The image of violence was so strong that merely lowering the sound was not held to make a great deal of difference. It was only when we removed the sound almost entirely that they felt the violence was lessened:

> *I think it was the swearing and the shouting that made it more violent.*
>
> *It's still violent, but it is not as bad.*
>
> *The sound definitely makes it worse. Nothing is the same without sound is it?*

Even so,

> *You get the violence from the facial expression as well.*

As we have seen before, this scene is difficult to edit to make it other than violent with a big V. Even by removing the sound, it could not be turned into little v. In the course of discussing *Deep Cover*, this group agreed that swearing could be violent, although not all did – swearing as violence is a far from settled matter.

> *I think swearing can, if it's threatening.*
>
> *It must be their attitude as well. If you just sat there and swore it wouldn't be the same as being nose to nose with somebody.*
>
> *It's the context – a lot of comedians swear and it's funny.*

The introduction of the term 'threatening' probably means (as discussed before in relation to the use of 'cunt') that for swearing to be violent it must offer a direct implication that violence will follow. The idea of 'nose to nose', however, does suggest that if the swearing intimidates, that too is violent. When swearing intimidates the effect is similar to actual violence, because the exercise of power by one person over another is involved.

Swearing, for this group, could be violent, but they did not consider that removing the word 'cunt', and substituting 'bitch', would have made the scene any less violent. To them it was the whole scene that was violent.

It was the whole way he was using language.

He could have been using any swear words really. That's what happens – that's how a man like that would react.

Although this was authentic violence, and set in a real world which this group could easily identify, this violence did not frighten them. Unlike *Deep Cover*, which they would not have watched, they said they would watch *Ladybird, Ladybird*, and some of them had:

That's the sort of thing I would watch – I've seen that.

We asked why.

Because it happens – it's real. You know it happens to other people.

I would be upset by it, but I would watch it.

It would upset me – it's the sort of thing you would discuss afterwards.

If it had a strong story line I would watch it.

This violence did not frighten them – while gangster violence in distant America did, because, as one of them said, 'You know it happens *to other people*'. Later in the discussion a similar comment was made: 'You can identify with her, *you can't imagine it happening to you*, but you do know it goes on'. While this group did fear 'street' violence, violence in the home was far removed from their experience, and screen versions of it did not have the power to frighten them. This was not the case with 'actuality' screen violence.

Violence on the doorstep

We showed the group the bomb blast scene from the documentary on the IRA. When asked, 'Is that violent?', they said, 'Yes, it's real'. It is interesting, however, that when we asked: 'What did you find the most violent bit?' 'the glass' was mentioned, and 'the woman screaming'. The blood (of which, admittedly, there was very little) did not feature: 'I didn't really notice that'. They asked us to edit, 'The child and the woman at the end', and this we did by taking out the close-up. Following the edit, they agreed that, 'You still got the gist of what was happening'. But did the edit make the scene less violent?

Yes.

I think it lessened the shock, not the violence.

Yes, it was less shocking.

This scene triggered thoughts of violence close to home, thoughts of 'visited violence'.

> *I think it's more shocking when it's close to home — like the Warrington bomb.*

We had overlooked the fact that we were in an area that had seen IRA activity, so at once we asked, 'When that happened did it make you more nervous about going out?' The answer was predictable, but not the extent of their nervousness. The bomb that destroyed the Arndale shopping centre in Manchester had been more than a year before, but even so:

> *I haven't been in Manchester since.*
>
> *I was very wary when I went [to Manchester].*
>
> *It made you more wary and more careful.*
>
> *If I was in Tesco or somewhere like that weeks later I was thinking about how I would get out if something like that happened.*

Discussing her emotional response to television programmes, one woman said that because she was pregnant, 'I find that things are bothering me more at the moment'. Prior to pregnancy she could stay in the room when certain programmes 'bothered' her, now they 'make me want to leave the room'. The programme, *Dawn till Dusk*, was singled out: 'I think you want to bring your baby into a safe world'. Commenting on her own pregnancy, another woman said: 'I was frightened of driving – I suppose you want to protect the baby'.

The shock of violence

Many different factors are at work in reaching a definition of violence, but the helplessness of the victim is a universal component. Shock is not a universal response to violence, but rather one of a number of features that may not be present for everyone, even though all agree that a scene is violent. The helplessness of the victim stands out as breaking the rules of social exchange, but shock is an emotional response to what is seen, which will differ between individuals. We are talking here about the grading of violence within generally accepted categories. No-one would be shocked by violence with a little v. Some might be shocked by big V and therefore consider it more violent. Those who were not shocked would not, on those grounds, move big V down to little v.

Definitions of violence seem to be independent of any shock factor. The definition of violence depends on what the protagonists are doing to each other and how they are doing it, not the viewer's emotional response to it. But, since it often is the viewer's response, shock should not be entirely overlooked in understanding of how viewers perceive violence.

War films and rules of violence

Some screen violence, like war films, does not break the rules governing violent behaviour, and indeed conforms to them. But violence in war is 'sanctioned violence', and the rules governing appropriate conduct are relaxed. For this reason, one does not apply moral judgements as one does in the case of *Ladybird, Ladybird* or *Deep Cover*. Yet it would be difficult to claim that *Full Metal Jacket*, *Platoon* or *The Deer Hunter* were not violent with a big V.

Many of the standard rules governing behaviour are carried over into war films. The killing of children, and to a lesser degree adult civilians, along with acts of cruelty, are still taboo. But when something is considered violent in a war film, it is usually realism that is the deciding element. The greater the belief that what is seen represents how it would really have been, then the more violent the scene is held to be. As in other film *genres*, the frontiers of violence in war films are constantly advanced by improvements in film-making technique.

6

Veterans of violence

Of the retired men drawn from social grades C2D, who formed one of our groups in Edinburgh, three, and possibly four, had seen action during the Second World War. Our recruitment criteria had not included this stipulation, but we were pleased at their presence since it allowed us to explore the relationship between the first-hand experience of war and screen portrayals of war. We discovered that they had seen combat when we asked:

> *What about people's own experience of violence – at first hand experience. Have you seen violence in pubs and places like that?*

> *I've seen real life violence in the army – in Normandy.*

We asked if he had seen the film, *The Longest Day*. He had, 'Two or three times'. We wanted his opinion on whether or not the film was realistic. He considered it was, but, judging by his later comments, it would seem that the realism must have referred to its accuracy as a document of an historical event, and not to the manner in which the violence was portrayed:

> *I think they should have done more on the horror side of it. This bravado with John Wayne, all the bravado, that was crap. I was scared – everybody was. There was nothing certain about coming back.*

The memory of violence past

At certain points, especially after seeing the footage from Bosnia, memories returned which these men had formerly repressed:

After the war you wanted to forget it but somehow as you get older you want to remember it. You want to go back to places where you were before and you want to relive things. I've been back to all the big places and there's only one thing I've got left to do and I'll do it sometime. As you get older you want to do it — I don't know if it's sentiment or what.

There is something inside you that makes you want to re-live it, it's strange.

I'm remembering some names tonight that I haven't thought about for 50 years.

We wanted to know whether their experience of war gave them different perceptions of screen violence. Could they help settle the question of desensitisation? If you have witnessed serious real-life violence, are you less sensitive to portrayed violence?

The most horrifying experience I ever had was during the invasion in Sicily. When we went ashore I saw bodies under their trucks burning — it was horrifying for an 18 year-old.

You got acclimatised to it though.

[Prompt] Do you get used to it in situations like that?

It was your life then. You got accustomed to it. The point is when you are in action you have not time to dwell on anything. You have to move on and look after number one.

I was at Normandy and I was in a prisoner of war camp and experienced some terrible things. I've never seen a war film yet that was realistic because only the people who were involved in these things know. People who make pictures don't know. They make pictures to sell. Over 50 years have gone by and I've never forgotten it.

Unfairness & violence

All the groups shown *Deep Cover* considered the violence realistic. Shown to these men, we had:

That was very violent — brutal.

[Prompt] What makes it violent? What particular aspect of it?

He looked like a psycho to me.

It wasn't a fair fight. He wasn't allowed to retaliate.

The blows that were delivered were realistic, but it's not entertainment.

[Prompt] Did it shock you?

I felt sorry for him.

Nothing can shock me nowadays.

You knew it wasn't real when you were watching it.

First hand experience of that sort of thing is more poignant than watching a hundred of them.

That's box office stuff — we know that.

Deep Cover was seen by this group as realistic, but not as real. But it was a passable rendering of violence — it was 'brutal', and real violence is brutal. They were not shocked by what they saw, although one did mention that he, 'felt sorry for him'. They may not have been shocked, but they did not approve of violence being portrayed in this way:

It doesn't give the producer an excuse to show such violence — he can imply it.

They did make edits:

I would leave in the first three hits with the stick and then I would edit the rest out because it got more brutal as it went on.

It was the crescendo of the violence that made it violent. They considered the scene still too violent, and asked for the faces of the onlookers to be removed:

I think the close-ups of the faces could do with being taken out.

This was done:

Yes, that's better.

It made the point still.

Although not shocked, these men could not see the entertainment value of such violence. The reason for not being shocked was their own experience of violence. The men who had seen combat claimed that only real violence is shocking, that is, where shock is taken as a jolt to the senses, and not shocking in the sense of being morally shocking:

If you see somebody bleeding in real life you remember that. I wouldn't remember that film five minutes later.

We asked them: 'if you had been brought up on a diet of very graphic violence, would you have felt less shocked by real life violence?'

No definitely not. It's absolutely different. It doesn't matter how many dead people you see — your're always shocked when you see the next one.

Violence in war films

Given that this group did not appreciate the violence in *Deep Cover*, and given the combat background of some of them, we wanted to know if violence in war films carried a different meaning from other forms of fictional violence. *The Longest Day* had been rounded on by some of these men because it portrayed battle action as violence with a little v, and thus, 'glorifies it':

I think these films glorify violence, but there's nothing glorious about it when you're there.

We asked had they seen *All Quiet on the Western Front.* They had. We asked if that was violent:

Yes, I would say it was very, very violent.

But they approved of the violence in that film:

These are actual facts which is a totally different thing to the films you are getting nowadays. At one time there was a story and violence was part of the story. Now I feel that there is violence and the story is part of the violence. A war film that is genuinely blood-thirsty I can understand but I can't understand these mindless films they now make.

We showed a clip from *Culloden* in which one of the Jacobites is slashed across the face and falls screaming to the ground. The camera returns to him more than once. One respondent considered that the sequence shown was 'quite violent', which prompted a response from one of the old soldiers:

To me there are two types of violence. There is the violence of war and I don't count that as violence, it acts as a warning. What I class as violence is the mindless stuff that you're getting on the box today which relates to nothing. It's just made for the sake of violence.

To which the same man added later:

To me war films are not violence — that is war, it's a separate item altogether.

In spite of these comments, these men did consider war films violent — indeed such films as *The Longest Day* and *All Quiet on the Western Front* were talked about in terms of the way they reflected the violence of war. But the respondents were making a distinction between the value of certain sorts of screen violence, basing their values on a comparison between screen and real life violence.

In discussing their early lives in Edinburgh and comparing them with today, they often said to how violent the streets had become. Comparing then and now, one man said:

It's a different kind of violence we have today. It's pretty mindless today. The Normandy Invasion was horrifying but it was necessary.

Referring to *The Longest Day*, one of them said:

It was a different type of violence. People nowadays are getting mugged — that's not violence, that's criminal.

This might appear confused reasoning, but it is not. Having themselves formed part of a vast machine of violence, they wanted to dissociate the violence in which they had participated from the violence of lawlessness. Their violence had been legitimate — 'horrifying, but it was necessary.' Basically, their violence had been good violence, whereas the civil violence of today is bad violence

Although *The Longest Day* was criticised for 'glorifying' war, and the violence of *All Quiet on the Western Front* approved of, there was a limit to how far they wanted the actual violence of war to be given space on the screen. When asked if war films should attempt to show the horrors he had witnessed, the person who had fought in Normandy, and had 'experienced some terrible things', replied:

No. I think the horrors are better kept to yourself.

Given their experiences, some of these men could not consider violence a fit subject for entertainment. *Pulp Fiction* was excluded from this because the violence was comic:

I found it comical — I couldn't stop laughing.

It wasn't violent, it was comical.

It was all dialogue.

It was too far-fetched to be believable.

The subject matter was not violence, but comic exchange. Experience had not made these men sensitive to violence – indeed, they were not shocked by violent imagery – but they wanted to have violence located in specific settings:

You could show more violence in war films because I feel it acts as a deterrent. It warns of what war is about.

But this was not a *carte blanche* to the producer to allow his imagination full rein. The new rules of injury did not find favour with these men. When applied to war, the new rules fell far short of capturing what happened on the battle ground. This group had seen real violence, and, as they said, screen violence and real violence are 'absolutely different'.

The legitimacy of violence

We have mentioned at several points that defining violence is not the same as accepting violence. In practice one cannot be totally separated from the other.

'Legitimate' real life violence was more readily accepted on film than 'bad' real life violence. Violence is easier to accept in a war film, since violence is a central feature of war, and is therefore naturally part of the narrative. The violence in *Deep Cover*, although perhaps part of a gangster's life, was not central to the story, and was therefore to some extent gratuitous. Violence of the *Deep Cover* type was seen as more violent that any equivalent violence in a war film.

To this extent, questions of taste, decency and the tolerance of violent images do play a part in defining screen violence, and cannot be ignored in exploring viewers' reactions to violence.

We were interested in the responses of this group – especially the veterans – to the scenes of destruction in Sarajevo and in Tusla. Did they define the sights seen as violence? In showing the market-place bombing in Sarajevo, we asked:

Is that violence?

No, not violence. It's gruesome, it's reality.

It's not glorified, it's fact. I find it tragic to watch, but it's fact.

We showed them the comments made by other groups, that the scene was not violent because action itself was absent, and that it was merely the aftermath of violence. They were not quite as unequivocal as other groups:

It's violence to an extent but it's got to be shown hasn't it.

It's the aftermath of violence.

We pressed on, showing the Reuters news feed:

You could have conveyed the same message with much less detail.

I'll always accept fact. I can watch news like that, but some people can't accept it if it's turned into a film.

If they turned it into a film they'd make it ten times more violent.

We asked if that was possible. Some considered it could, but others thought differently:

I don't think you could make anything more gruesome than that.

Okay, but you could make it longer.

Here again, prolonging a scene is held to increase its violence. In this case, although the scene was merely the aftermath of violence, it was still considered that the horror could be heightened by making the scene longer.

Most groups came close to defining the aftermath of violence as itself violent. They found difficulty in not categorising scenes of injury as violent, and it was almost as if they felt they were demeaning the victims. The feelings provoked by the aftermath of violence are the same as the feelings provoked by viewing the injuries as they occur. Lingering close-ups of injuries were seen to be 'gruesome'; lingering shots of the injuries being delivered were seen as violent. The feelings generated in each case seemed to be the same. The scenes shown from Bosnia showed terrible and shocking injury. The footage from Belfast showed the moment of explosion, but hardly any injury. Many respondents felt that to define the Belfast scene as violent, and not the Bosnia clip, was captious.

Overall, however, the opinion was that the Bosnia scenes were not 'violent', since the actual act of violence was not witnessed.

7

Keeping up appearances

The sample group of women aged over 60 was drawn from social grades BC1 and lived in Bristol. Their world was strikingly different from that of the over-60 year-old men in Edinburgh, who were drawn from social grades C2D. When asked for their preferred programmes, they mentioned travel programmes, wildlife, and natural history programmes, along with 'good drama'.

They did not like 'Cops and robbers – *the Bill* and things like that'. One woman said, 'There are too many crime type programmes'. *Crimewatch*, however, was enjoyed. In the course of a brief discussion of *Crimewatch*, one woman said, 'I like all documentaries' – expressing a preference for programmes that deal with real life:

> *I like it when they spend a whole week at a hospital and do different reports on people every day. That's real life – I can relate to those.*

We wanted to compare this group with the group recruited because of its fear of crime. We asked if they feared crime at all.

They were not nervous of being the victims of crime in the same way, or to the same degree, as those specially recruited for their fear of crime, but they had reservations about venturing abroad on their own to certain locations, and were nervous when confronted by certain situations:

> *I'm nervous. I've just been to the dentist and I had to walk from the village and there were several men coming towards me which made me nervous. I haven't been out on my own much in the dark and I did feel nervous.*
>
> *I think it's changed over the last five or 10 years. There was a time when I would go into town at night and park my car in a multi-*

storey car park on my own. I wouldn't do that now – no way. I never used to think twice about it.

I find it quite creepy if you're walking towards the centre of town – even if there's two or three of you together. I do tend to look over my shoulder.

These seem reasonable fears, given their age. Their nervousness was based on a reasoned calculation of danger. If they were at times nervous on leaving the house, none said she was nervous at home. All had partners, but then so did the 'nervous' women, who were considerably younger than the members of this group.

Personal taste and violence

These respondents claimed they had similar tastes in programmes to their partners, apart from sport and violence. We asked if they ever went to the cinema. Some did, but only occasionally. *The Full Monty* was declared 'brilliant'. When asked, 'What was the last film you saw?', *Oscar Wilde* was mentioned by one woman. She had not enjoyed it:

I didn't like it particularly. I didn't think they had enough of his home life with his wife. It concentrated too much on the homosexual affair. It was done very tastefully though and I think the acting was good. I think they could have shown more about his children and his home.

Dislike of violence

As usual, we began the viewing with the clip from *Thief Takers*.

I could watch that because it was all happening. It wasn't nearly as tense as when you see somebody coming up the stairs with a knife and waiting for something to happen. It's all make believe.

I agree with you there – your're not kept in suspense.

I thought it was violent but it was as it should be for that kind of programme.

'Playful violence', not to be taken seriously? One woman did not think it was violent:

Frankly I just thought how stupid it was. Most of it was unreal. And there's always a pretty woman doing absolutely nothing.

The only part that was seen as violent was the head-butting, not the shooting. Asked why, one person replied:

I don't know, it always upsets me.

We asked if head-butting upset them more than watching someone punch someone: 'Yes, I think so', to which someone else added: 'I didn't like it either'. They wanted the head-butting scene to be edited, and once this was done it was declared to be 'definitely better'. It is interesting that the term 'upset' was used in the context of defining violence. These respondents had no taste for violence. And why should they? Violence stands in opposition to gentleness and the regular ordering of life. Perhaps that is why one person did not especially enjoy *Oscar Wilde*, and wished the film had given more space to Wilde's 'home life with his wife' rather than the world of rent boys and homosexual fops.

The group was shown only the edited version of *Deep Cover*, and, not surprisingly, they considered it extremely violent. This was in part because 'It could really be happening':

This one looks as though it could really be happening. The other one was a fantasy programme to me.

There's a close-up on this one.

You find that is frightening because it's credible — it could happen. You could get someone who goes berserk.

The first one [Thief Takers] was just a film whereas this one could actually have been a camera taking shots of something real.

This group felt this clip to be powerfully violent because it managed to create the feeling that it was actuality. The group asked for several edits. They first asked for the thumps and the victim's screams to be removed. When they saw this version they said it didn't help, as the scene was still credible. A second edit restored the sound, but at a reduced level. This revision was altered visually, removing the majority of the blows, leaving the reactions of the witnesses. On completing these edits there were several comments:

I think that's O.K.

You still get the idea that's he's been thrashed to bits but it's not too violent.

If you're watching that type of film you still want to see some action, otherwise there is no point in watching it.

[Prompt] So that was better?

Yes, much.

You can hear the sound, you can see the horror on their faces — you can imagine the rest.

Yes, you've just got to use your imagination.

The interesting point is that although they did not like violence, they did not object to action. They even enjoyed it. But they did not enjoy violence. So they simply stripped away the violent components, leaving only what they saw as acceptable action.

They found the scene especially violent because it was set in what they could imagine was the real world:

Why you find that frightening is because it's credible — it could happen. You could get somebody going berserk.

If we now look at the responses of this group to domestic violence, we see that in this case they made even closer comparisons between the screen world and their own world.

Offence & violence

The group of 'nervous' women did not find the domestic violence clips disturbing, because in their own domestic background nothing threatening existed. For the over 60s group, the violence seen in *Ladybird, Ladybird* was disturbing, not in the sense of creating fear, but because it was vulgar and gratuitous:

That's violence for the sake of violence.

The language was just for the sake of using it — it doesn't add to the story.

It's the sort of thing you'd shut off.

I find that quite offensive. To be honest it demeans the people of Liverpool and he just comes over as an absolute male chauvinist pig.

There were two people when I went to the doctor's surgery last week and he was using the most dreadful language — I thought he was going to hit her. I was quite shocked by it.

Did it surprise you because it was in your area? Would you have been so shocked if it had been in St Paul's [a rough district of Bristol]?

Possibly I wouldn't have been so surprised . . . I've never seen anybody around my area behaving like that and shouting in public.

For women of this age and social group, to draw attention to oneself in public by loud display is to break the accepted rules, and is the antithesis of respectability. When the members of this group discussed the language used by the assailant in *Deep Cover*, one person said that she would expect the use of 'the F word' in such a scene because, 'That's the type of person who would use those sorts of words'.

For these respondents, individuals represent more than just themselves: they stand for the groups to which they belong. The neighbourhoods in which the members of this group live are characterised by good manners and order. To quote one woman again: 'I've never seen anybody around my area behaving like that and shouting in public'.

This group was interesting because it employed judgements about screen portrayals of life not employed by other groups. But did these judgements influence their definition of violence? Referring to *Ladybird, Ladybird*, we asked, 'What for you was the most violent bit in it?'

When he was kicking her and the fact that children were watching.

I found that very upsetting.

The language

[Prompt] Can language itself be a form of violence?.

I think so, yes.

[Prompt] Can you have verbal violence?

Yes you can. I don't think it's necessary.

[Prompt] If there is no physical violence can it still be violence if he's just swearing at her?

Yes.

We asked if they wanted some of the swearing to be edited out:

It could offend you as much as watching the violence.

There are about 25 swear words in the scene, and cutting was difficult, but we did shorten the scene:

It doesn't get any better does it?

It's still very violent.

We then tried to help by saying:

He sits on the sofa and we hear the 'C word' and two 'F words' – would you take those out?

They wanted to, but one woman observed:

I think that sort of language comes from the type of person he is – you accept it.

[Prompt] So you'd leave the language in?

Maybe not so much of it because he goes on and on.

Would you make the sound less at the point where he hits her in the face?

They agreed that to lower the sound would be better, but one woman said:

The actual content is so horrible anyway that whatever you do it's not going to make any difference.

It was not an easy clip to edit, and impossible to edit to make the 'hard' violence 'soft' violence. After showing various edited versions it emerged that, although everything about the clip was violent, it was the outburst of violence with the initial thump that made the greatest impression – 'I think that initial thump is the one you feel, even though you're expecting it'. This group perceived the violence in this scene to be violence with a big V, even massive V. And for them taste was a contributory factor in perceiving violence: 'The swearing offends as much as watching the violence'.

It was difficult to get the members of this group to separate what they considered violent from what they found distasteful: it was all one abhorrent whole. With a previous group we discussed at some length how swearing could be considered violent, even though no physical injury is inflicted. That group held that language could be violent because it instilled fear.

In this group there was no reference to fear, and instead the conversation concentrated on the offence the swearing gave: 'It offends as much as watching violence', and, 'I don't think it's necessary' are two examples.

Bad language undermining comedy

If we now turn to *Pulp Fiction* we see that although the language was considered distasteful, the scene itself was not considered violent, and for the usual reason – that it was funny, although not all that funny for these women. Indeed, for some of the group the level of swearing robbed the clip of comic impact. (Perhaps taste is making an indirect contribution to a definition of violence here. If someone's tastes are such that they object profoundly to what they see, then the objection may rob a scene of its harmless nature, and transform into violence what for others is not violent.)

We showed the shooting scene in the car, and asked: 'Was that violent?'

I wouldn't say it was violent.

It was quite comical actually – he was so casual about it.

I could put up with the violence, but what I do find irritating is that everything that is a little bit violent has to have rotten language with it. Why must it always have awful language in it? Just the violence on its own, I would sit there and think, 'well, they're only acting' and a lot of it could wash over me. But that I do find horrible.

[Prompt] One of you found it amusing, did anyone else?

Well, it was very casual.

I just think those things are rubbish.

I thought it was stupid.

[Prompt] Did it make any anybody want to laugh?

No, not really.

It's the language that I think is so unnecessary. They use it like 'hello' and 'goodbye'.

[Prompt] Did the language make it amusing?

No – it was the way they did it . . . the swearing most definitely ought to be edited from the scene.

Any amusement that this scene provided for these respondents derived from the 'casual' way that Marvin, the passenger in the back, was shot. In contrast to the other groups, the swearing was not seen as adding to the humour of the scene, and instead detracted from it. Without the swearing the scene would have been entirely different. It is doubtful whether, for most people, it would have been amusing at all. Yet this group wanted the swearing removed – it was 'so unnecessary'.

8

The boys next door

We have discussed already how 'hard' men in London defined screen violence, and explained that they were recruited on the basis of their familiarity with violence. The recruitment questionnaire (see Appendix 2) allowed us to select them as likely to have engaged in violent behaviour on a reasonably frequent basis.

The 'hard' men were single, aged 18-24, and we wanted to compare how they defined violence with how other men, of the same age, but who were not 'hard', defined violence.

As a shorthand, we called this sample 'soft', but 'soft' really means no more than 'not hard'. They were not recruited for gentleness, sensitivity or an abhorrence of violence, or any other quality one might associate with the term 'soft'. When asked if they ever came across violence, they said that they had. We asked this question not just as a way of enquiring into their exposure to violence, and reactions to it, but as a way of checking whether the sample fitted the recruitment specifications.

Violent in real life, violent on the screen

They had come across violence:

> *Now and again, yes.*
>
> *There are fights in clubs most weeks — it depends where you go.*
>
> *[Prompt] Do you get involved in them yourself?*
>
> *Not if I can help it.*
>
> *There are many people looking for it and they tend to congregate in*

the same areas, so if you want to have a good night out without getting your head kicked in it's wise to go somewhere that it's not likely to happen.

These men avoided trouble in a way the 'hard' men did not. One or two of these respondents claimed to have seen 'really violent' fights. We asked, 'What made it nasty?'

The presence of knives and it wasn't fair — people were ganging up on one person.

If we compare this with the comments they made in response to the unedited version of *Deep Cover*, we see a remarkable similarity between their real-life values and their screen values. The clip was deemed to be 'a lot more gruesome' than *Thief Takers*:

You were close up.

The violence wasn't instant — he was suffering.

It was a bit unfair.

Again — and we cannot press this point enough — what constitutes violence on the screen is measured against real life. One is recognised from the other. What is not so obvious is the process of transferring values from the real world to the screen.

Losing oneself in the film

Viewers tend to 'lose themselves' in a story. After watching the unedited version of *Deep Cover*, which all agreed was violent, one person in this group said he had enjoyed watching the beating:

I thought it was good, yes.

[Prompt] What did you like about it?

It was quite real — you actually felt you were there. That's what I like about films.

Were you involved in it?

Yes, I like films that you can get involved in.

The fight scene in *Deep Cover* was made real by a variety of narrative devices, like the close-up shots of injury, and the spray of blood from the helpless victim's mouth. To give the viewer a surgeon's-eye-view of an injury gives a documentary 'feel' to violence. Such stark realism implies 'this is not a representation of violence, this is violence, and because this is violence – actual violence as in real life – then it is to be judged by values drawn from real life'.

By using 'the new rules of injury', the producer pulls a double trick. The depicted violence looks shocking, indeed it is exaggerated to give the appearance of being more real than the real. Furthermore, as we have argued, the producer is the viewer's only authority for what looks real, because most people have never witnessed serious violence.

Because screen violence is seen as real, it is seen as shocking. Because the viewer is caught up in the film emotionally, he or she applies the values by which violence is judged in real life. One of these is that violence is wrong when enacted against a helpless person. By using very graphic, 'realistic' images of injury, the producer 'ups the emotional ante', strengthening the engagement of an uncritical viewer with his film.

9

The girls next door

If we compare the female equivalent of the men just discussed, they agree about what makes something violent. But having defined something as violent, their response to it is not the same. For example, this group of women aged 18-24 showed a lower tolerance to violence than did their male counterparts. Unlike the men, they did not enjoy violence.

> *[Prompt] Do you ever go and see violent films?*
>
> *I went to see one on Sunday actually which I didn't want to see, but my husband persuaded me to go. It was called Face Off with John Travolta . . . It was very violent. I don't see the need for violence in films. Strong violence puts me off.*

Non-enjoyment of violence

Does the tolerance, or even acceptance, of violence influence what people define as violence?

At the margins, it probably does. If something is judged to be on the borderline between being violent with a big V and little v, then disapproval would influence the decision. However, if there is no doubt that the violence is violence with a big V, it would be classed as violence with a big V whether one disapproved or not.

The women in this group did not find violence entertaining. They were similar to the older women discussed earlier – violence upset them. One participant jumped every time any sudden violent action came on the screen. They had not witnessed much real life violence, although one woman reported: 'Years ago I was in Worcester and I saw a guy getting beaten up and I cried. I got really upset'. We moved quickly to the scene from *Thief Takers*. We asked if the scene was violent.

Absolutely.

Yes.

I didn't find that violent.

I don't see how anybody could get any enjoyment watching something like that.

The best bit about that was the tension — that something could happen to them. It was the build-up that gets your interest. You just don't know what's going on.

[Prompt] Why did you think it wasn't violent?

Because it's intense. I've seen the programme and it's very good — I liked it. There was a story there. You get into the story. That wasn't too violent for me.

[Prompt] What made it violent for you?

The shooting. I can't understand the mentality of a person who would get pleasure out of watching something like that. I can't understand why they needed to do that. You can have a good storyline without having a load of people getting shot.

[Prompt] What was the most violent bit?

When that guy got shot in the back. You know he's been shot because you can see the blood pouring out of his jacket, but it doesn't seem realistic, to be honest.

[Prompt] If it is not realistic how is it horrible?

It just is.

The sequence was edited, cutting away before the slow motion shot of the bullets and blood leaving the back of the victim.

[Prompt] Does that make it better?

A little bit better, yes.

[Prompt] What about you?

It [the edit] didn't spoil it for me.

[Prompt] But did it add to it by having it taken out?

No.

[Prompt] What about the head-butt? Did that seem violent?

Yes.

That was more violent — it's personal contact.

I find that more violent than going out and stabbing somebody.

[Prompt] Have you ever seen a head-butt?

No.

I agree — it was personal contact and you thought, 'God, that must have hurt'.

When it's personal they really mean it and it's aggressive.

[Prompt] Would you like the head-butt taken out or the sound of the head-butt?

The sound.

I think the music makes it more violent as well.

But it sets the atmosphere so you really need it.

The edit was done, and the clip re-run with the sound of the head-butt removed. Although the exaggerated sound effect of head on head had disturbed them, the remaining visual was still unacceptable:

No, that spoilt it.

The group then decided to remove the action entirely:

That's better.

Yes, it was.

Before commenting, let us look at their responses to the violence in *Deep Cover*. We first showed the cinema version, let them edit it, and then showed the version that went out on Carlton Television. After showing the cinema version we started by asking: 'Was that violent?'

Oh yes.

That was violent.

[Prompt] Did you enjoy it at all?

No I didn't. If I knew that was in there I wouldn't watch the film.

[Prompt] What made it particularly violent?

The way he was smacking him on the head.

The blood spurting out.

It was reality — that sort of thing does go on.

It was more realistic than the last one we saw.

[Prompt] What made it realistic?

The guy was defenceless and you normally find in everyday crime the person is defenceless.

The acting was really good there compared to the last one.

[Prompt] So the blood spraying out was violent. Would you take that out? How could we lessen the violence there? What actually constitutes the violence?

I think it was the sound of the thud.

Even if you cover your eyes you know what's happening so it makes you cringe.

The bloke screaming.

I think if you took the blood out it wouldn't be realistic.

If you'd been hit over the head with a baseball bat blood is bound to come out.

[Prompt] Would you keep as many shots in?

I didn't like the close-up of his face.

How about the swearing?

No. You hear that language wherever you go now.

I think he should look more injured because people will think that they can go out and hit people like that and they're still going to be conscious.

The group edited the scene more severely than Carlton Television. After the initial two blows in wide shot, their version consisted of the reaction shots with the sound off, and the off-camera blows removed until the very end when two of the quieter thumps were used.

That was much better because you know what's going on, but you don't actually have to see it.

[Prompt] Would you tone it down more?

The sound makes you cringe, but then you need that if you're not seeing the pictures. I prefer to hear the sound than see it.

[Prompt] There are other ways of doing this — we could just have the faces and have the sound taken off. Would that work? Shall we give it a go? Shall we take it all off but the first bit — you need to see it once don't you?

I don't know whether that would work.

I don't think it would.

You can't leave it all to the imagination — you need something to stimulate your thinking.

The group was then offered a version which consisted entirely of the reaction shots and the sound. This was to see how much could be removed without the scene losing its meaning entirely. The response was mixed:

Better.

Yes, that was good.

No, I think you need a few of the punches. You need to see what he's doing to his face.

Having reduced the scene from its unacceptably violent cinema version in a variety of ways, the group were shown the Carlton Television edited version:

I think that was about half and half.

It doesn't focus on him for too long.

You know what's going on — I think that's good.

[Prompt] So seeing the repeat violence, is that bad for you?

Yes, you don't need to see it over and over again. It can get too much.

Why watch violence?

In this group we found not simply a statement of what made each clip violent, but an attitude towards violence in general that was less pronounced in the other groups. Their definition of violence was overlaid with an emotional response to what was seen. They also questioned the morality of depicting violence at all. For example, the statement — 'I can't understand the mentality of a person who could get pleasure out of watching something like that' – is not just a statement about the level of violence, but a judgement about its moral value, and more, a judgement about the moral worth of somebody who found such violence entertaining.

Furthermore, the scene where one of the diners is shot in the back, and blood spurts from holes in his suit, lacked one of the key components of screen violence – realism. And this group, too, did not consider it 'realistic'. But they did consider it horrible, and when asked why it was horrible, if it wasn't realistic, the reply was: 'It just is'.

We get a clue to how this group viewed violence if we go to *Deep Cover* and the quotation above, 'You don't need to see it over and over again. It can get too much' – referring to the beating. Such violence 'just is' distasteful, so distasteful that it made at least one woman 'cringe'. Referring to *Deep Cover*, she said:

Even if you cover your eyes up you know what's happening so it makes you cringe.

Even so, it was thought better to hear acts of violence rather than to confront them directly:

The sound makes you cringe, but then you need that if you're not seeing the pictures. I prefer to hear the sound than see it.

This group was the only one which pushed the 'Playful violence' of *Thief Takers* – just – over the borderline from little v to big V. But they did not differ from other groups in their criteria of what makes something violent. Throughout the showing of various clips they pointed to factors like aggression, close personal contact, unfairness, the helplessness of the victim, and the length of a violent sequence. But in one respect they did differ from the other groups. To them, a scene did not have to be 'realistic' to qualify as violence.

Nearly 100 people took part in the editing process, and only in a few members of this group did we come across this extreme sensitivity to violence. Even the group specially recruited for their fear of crime did not show this kind of sensitivity.

Sensibilities & violence

This group was shocked by seeing violence – of almost any kind – and they defined most of the clips as violent. People in other groups often found violence distasteful, but they retained an analytical judgement about whether or not something really qualified as violence. This group assessed violence as much by their emotional response to it as by analytical yardsticks.

But not every clip was defined as strong violence. *Pulp Fiction* was not defined by this group as violent, and we showed both the scene in the car where the brains are splattered over the occupants, and also the scene where a needle is stabbed into the chest of a woman who has overdosed on heroin. Even with this group, the comic element in *Pulp Fiction* acted as protection. Also, *Culloden* was not seen as violent, although we showed both a battle scene of a Jacobite slashed across the face and falling, moaning, to the ground, and the hunting down of a family by British soldiers, with the subsequent killing of not just the menfolk, but the women and children as well. This was not seen as violent. One person said, feelingly:

> *It is violent, but I don't personally find it offensive.*

The reason it was not offensive, and why the violence was accepted, was given another person:

> *Yes, that was violent. The voice-over made it real – it was more of a documentary.*

For them, *Culloden* did not fall into the category of violence with a big V, but then neither did it for any of the groups. The interesting point, however, is that it was not found violent because it had the appearance of a documentary. After watching *Ladybird, Ladybird*, one woman discussed the film biography of the singer Tina Turner. Although the Tina Turner film was considered extremely violent, the violence was accepted, although the violence in the Turner film was considered much stronger than *Ladybird, Ladybird*:

> *I sat and watched that film the whole way through and I cried at the end. It made me feel sick, but it was a true story. Because it was true I was fascinated to see that someone could go through all that and get to where she has. He was hitting her while he was actually raping her.*

It was a true story and that was what she went through. I expected to see that before I watched it.

Presumably the members of this group who had seen the film, *The Krays*, had again expected to see violence, but once more the violence was defended on the grounds of authenticity – it had really happened. Asked if they would want to edit *The Krays*, one reply was:

No. I think because it's a real life film – that is what they got up to.

Although sensitive to violence, these women are not 'revolted' by violence, provided it had a point beyond pure entertainment. Films such as *Culloden* do not 'revolt', and nor do films about real life happenings. Both Tina Turner and *The Krays* had an informative documentary quality because they were based on fact.

These respondents openly admitted to being sensitive to suffering, and did say that their emotions came into play in defining something as violent. After viewing the destruction of the Highland family in *Culloden*, it was agreed that this was violent because, 'You feel sorry for the family'. Someone else said, 'I wouldn't say that it's the violence that upsets you, it's the emotion.' We said, 'So in fact when you define something as violent your emotions come into it', and they agreed.

Before showing the clip of the drunk hitting the Teddy Bear thief, we could guess what their responses must have been on hearing of Lady Diana's death, and we were not wrong: 'Disbelief'; 'Shock'; 'Very upset'. 'When her brother was speaking at the funeral I couldn't stop crying'. 'Even when it was shown repeatedly I cried every time because I felt so sorry for them all – her kids especially. I wondered how I would cope at their age without a mum. Putting yourself in their situation really touched me'.

Their responses to the news clip were fairly similar to those of other groups. They did not consider it very violent:

It wasn't violent. I could understand why he did it because I was getting angry with him. He [the thief] was kind of smirking and it irritated me.

I think he got off fairly lightly actually. It didn't do him any harm.

Referring to the violence, one respondent said:

It didn't offend me at all. It was just a piece of news as far as I was concerned. It quite amused me in some respects because the guy was so drunk.

This group displayed considerable sensitivity to the sight of suffering, pain or injury. What really offended them was violence that had no point other than entertainment – violence to keeping the narrative going, as in *Thief Takers*. Apart from this, they do not differ from other groups in constructing definitions of violence. But when faced with violence as entertainment, they were revolted, and revulsion did indeed make violence seem stronger to them than to other groups. We do not know how widespread such sensitivity is, only that it exists.

10

Women with children at home

It is not surprising that being a parent with children living at home influences attitudes towards violence. We wanted to know whether having children influenced the definition of what is a violent programme. We did not want to know what violent material they would allow their children to watch, but whether the simple fact of having children made a difference to how violence was defined. Did parents with children living at home differ from others in their definitions of what constituted violence?

We began by looking at women aged 25 to 45, social grades BC1, whose eldest child was aged five to 11, all of whom came from Edinburgh or the neighbouring areas. Unlike the previous group, they were fairly tolerant of violence, and even enjoyed it. Both *Cracker* and *Taggart* were named as programmes that they liked to watch. Although *Taggart* was not defined as violent, *Cracker* was:

> *Cracker can be very violent - I just really enjoy it. I sometimes find the violence very disturbing, but I feel it's within the context.*
>
> *Do you think there's too much violence on television?*
>
> *There's different types of violence.*

We asked this woman to 'classify the different types'. She did not really do so, but in the course of discussing violence said:

> *There is well made violence.*
>
> *[Prompt] What's well made violence?*
>
> *Well, in something like* Cracker *where they bring it into the storyline and you can see the reason behind it. That's different*

from seeing a cop beating people up and everybody going around shooting.

The influence of parenthood

Having established that they were tolerant of violence if it could be seen as part of a story line, we asked if they had ever experienced violence in real life. The account given by one of the participants suggested that having children might affect one's response to violence.

> *I was coming out of a restaurant and there was a group of five guys in the street and this car with tinted windows came up and six guys with baseball bats jumped out and started beating these other guys up and we couldn't get past. I just went for this guy with my bag and the gang leader who was standing by the car told them to get back in the car. I stayed with these guys until the ambulance came.*

Puzzled by such foolhardy action, and by the audacity of her attack, we asked: 'What made you launch into them?'

> *Because I've got a son of the same age and you just can't stand by and watch somebody being beaten up. To be honest I didn't think. But when the police said did I want to go and give evidence in court I said no thank you very much. We just gave them the car number.*

We asked her how upsetting she found the violence and injury she witnessed:

> *Well the ambulance came and he wasn't too badly hurt, but I was quite hyped up afterwards.*

> *[Prompt] Did the injuries look different to the injuries you see on television?*

> *Actually, there was less blood.*

Feeling sorry for the victim

We showed *Thief Takers* to the group, and there was nothing remarkable about their responses. Like nearly everyone, they saw it as 'Playful violence':

> *It was supposed to appear violent, but it didn't.*

> *You were very conscious that it was just a bunch of actors.*

They defined the violence as: 'A lot of action I think'. They did consider *Deep Cover* to show serious violence, but there was nothing in their responses to suggest that being a parent affected their judgement. One woman wanted to edit:

[from] the minute he has him on the table. I couldn't look after that. He couldn't get up and go anywhere.

Context was important for these women, who were interested in what the victim might have done to deserve the beating:

I think if he'd done something awful in the film I would probably have thought he'd got what he deserved, but if it was just some poor wee soul that was getting beaten up I would have flinched more.

Once more, the respondents' emotional reactions were important in making the violence more or less acceptable. But a lack of sympathy for the victim does not necessarily lessen the sense of violence – it just makes it seem more 'just', or less unjust. One woman offered a hint that there might be a relationship between parenthood and attitudes to violence. She said that before judging the level of the violence one needed to know if he had 'done something awful':

That's right, if he'd murdered a child or whatever – it would depend on what he had done.

At their suggestion, we had already made a cut where the assailant comes round the table to deliver a further beating. We asked: 'Do you want us to go further and take some more out of it?' The same respondent said again:

I don't know, it depends on what he's done.

One woman mentioned that she had an 11 year-old child living in the family, and a 19 year old boy away at college. We asked if she thought her 19 year-old would enjoy the uncut version of *Deep Cover*.

I know he would because he likes these types of film. He's a film buff, he's doing a course on filming.

I may be wrong but it seems to be a male trait. My son is coming up for 12 and he enjoys watching these sort of things.

My husband would enjoy it. There are films that we get out together to watch, but there are films that he would watch on his own.

[Prompt] Does it bother you that your husband likes these films?

No – if that's what he enjoys watching that's fine.

I think there are definitely films that men enjoy watching more than women.

The fact that these women saw this difference between themselves and their menfolk suggests that sex is more important in the response to violence than being a parent. We saw in the other groups that women use the same criteria as men to define violence, but they differ in their enjoyment of it. There is no reason to suppose that, because they are mothers, these women define violence differently from women without children.

Violence involving children

If being a parent does not affect the general definition of violence, there is one specific area where it does have an effect, namely violence involving children. This brings us back to the reason why the woman decided to face a gang of thugs bent on beating someone of her own son's age – she could imagine her own son being attacked. It is similar with screen violence involving children. We discussed the domestic violence scene of *Brookside*, and began by asking: 'Was that violent?'

Yes.

Very violent.

Disturbingly violent.

It wasn't explicit with lots of blood, but you knew it was violent.

[Prompt] How could you make it less violent?

I don't think you would want to make it less violent. It would detract from the whole storyline.

I think it's important to show stuff like that on television.

[Prompt] So you wouldn't want it sanitised?

Not at all.

Lots of kids are seeing domestic violence every day whether they like it or not so it's quite important to get these things out into the open.

We followed this with *Ladybird, Ladybird*:

That was very much more violent than the other.

[Prompt] What made it particularly violent?

The kids watching.

[Prompt] How did the kids make it violent?

Because most violence is towards the woman but here the violence is towards them as well. The fact that they're witnessing it makes it more violent.

Seeing their father acting in that way is awful.

[Prompt] Do you think women who don't have children would feel as strongly about it as you do?

I think it would still affect people.

The expressions on the children's faces would still affect people. It's shocking because it's tea-time as well. A lot of people have this conception that domestic violence takes place behind closed doors late at night but this is the middle of the day.

The scene was so normal – it was somebody's sitting room.

And it seemed like there was no provocation.

We asked if the violence 'seemed worse because there's no provocation'. They agreed it did, but it was clear it was the presence of the two children that really made the scene seem more violent – a reaction possibly related more to parenthood rather than to sex.

Respondents in other groups had said that the presence of the children was disturbing, but, asked if that made the scene more violent, said not. This group of women was different, and they did think that the violence was heightened: 'The fact that they were witnessing it makes it more violent'.

Normality of the setting

Perhaps more than any other group, the women in this group were impressed by the normality of the setting:

It's shocking because it's at tea-time as well.

The scene was so normal – it was somebody's sitting room.

This was not pool-room violence, but a man venting his anger on a woman and children who deserved his protection. In the course of the physical violence, he screams, 'Fuck you and fuck the kids, fuck the lot of you'. Not surprisingly, the women viewed the scene with shocked attention. They were shocked, as one woman said, 'Because it's close to home'. As far as we could tell, it was not close to their own homes, but it was close to their thoughts of home.

Practically all our respondents saw the presence of the children as making the scene more disturbing. Editing the children out was not thought to reduce the violence of the scene, but violence can often be achieved by devices that have little to do with the actual act of violence – low lighting, foreboding music and so on. Just such an impression was achieved in the case of *Ladybird, Ladybird* by the presence of the children, and by having the violence set in an ordinary house, not a slum or a palace. These devices can all help to make the violence more disturbing and reinforce the conclusion that something is violent.

In summary, being mothers with children living at home made no real difference to how the members of this group defined violence in general. It made a difference only when the violence touched on factors directly relating to them as mothers. As an end-note it is worth mentioning that they did not want the scene edited at all. The protection of children was important to them, and they saw *Ladybird, Ladybird* as an important film because it showed domestic violence in all its horror.

11

Men with children at home

Very little space will be given to the group of men aged 25 to 45, drawn from social grades C2D, since virtually all the points they made have been covered by the other groups. Like the husbands of the women in the previous group, these men showed a distinctively 'masculine' appreciation of violent scenes. One man, for example, said:

I've got a laser disc player — a lot of the films you get nowadays are car chases and crashes and people getting wasted. I love the special effects in them.

The non-effect of parenthood

We could find no evidence that being a parent with children living at home influenced their definition of violence, although, unlike the women whose eldest children were between five and 11, this group's eldest children were between 12 and 16. It seems unlikely, but there might therefore have been a difference in protective feeling as a result of the age difference. The influence of fatherhood was not absent from their responses to images of violence, but it had no apparent bearing on definitional issues. For example, after watching *Thief Takers*, they volunteered that it should go out only after the nine o'clock watershed. They themselves did not find it violent, but said:

I think that would definitely have to be shown after nine o'clock.

I wouldn't let my lad see that — he's 12. He'd be running round the house smashing everything up — that's what he used to do a few years ago.

An anxiety not to over-excite their children was echoed by other members of the group:

It gets them going doesn't it?

Yes, it winds them up.

There was no absence of parental concern for the well-being of their children on the part of these men. In the mothers' group, the only difference made by being a parent was in their response to domestic violence. We shall concentrate on that area with the fathers to see if similar processes might be at work in how violence is defined.

We showed *Ladybird, Ladybird* before the wife-battering scene from *Brookside*:

That was awful – the language, the violence.

That's sad. It's not enjoyable.

Unfortunately though it's everyday life for some people. It makes you more aware of what's happening.

[Prompt] What made that so violent?

A man hitting a woman.

The kids being there.

It is almost like a documentary. It's almost fly on the wall. You could imagine that being real life.

You can actually believe that that happened when you watch it.

I would believe that was real.

[Prompt] Let's just look at it again.

Everything going on is real isn't it?

She knows what's going to happen.

[Prompt] What makes it so real?

Everything in the house – the curtains, the everyday things.

That's an everyday occurrence in some houses.

What bothers me is that actors or not, those children were actually watching that. That would frighten me – innocent kids are watching that.

I wouldn't let my kids watch that.

It shouldn't be filmed for video, television or anything else.

We know it goes on but so does paedophilia, are we going to film that as well? It's unacceptable.

[Prompt] *We've shown that to a couple of women's groups, and it's bothered you more than the women.*

That's what I mean. I know a woman that it's been happening to, but until you see something like that you don't realise what she's going through. It's clicked something for me.

But does a film company have to make money out of it?

I don't think they've made it to make money — they made it to show everyday life.

[Prompt] *The women that we've talked to found it disturbing, but your reaction seems much stronger. Is it because you're blokes? What the women were saying is that it hadn't happened to them, but that they could imagine it happening with a different bloke, so they could put themselves in that position.*

I think you find it disgusting.

You don't think it could be you doing it but subconsciously. I think you feel a bit ashamed because it's a bloke doing it to a woman.

[Prompt] *If you wanted to tone it down, how would you do it?*

Take the kids out.

You couldn't tone it down.

[Prompt] *Okay, the kids are now out. Does it make much of a difference not having the kids in?*

The violence is still the same, but you're not seeing the petrified looks on the kid's face.

But the looks on the kid's face are there for a reason.

It helps a bit but it doesn't make much difference.

[Prompt] *Do you think it's because you've got kids . . .?*

Certainly for me, yes.

[Prompt] *Do you think lads of 18 who haven't got kids would have taken them out?*

I don't know.

I think everyone would say take the kids out.

Following this discussion we ran the domestic violence scene from *Brookside*. We will provide the responses to that, and then comment on both together. We showed the wife battering in *Brookside*:

It's more acceptable.

There wasn't all the f-ing and blinding.

There was a lot more verbal abuse in the other one.

[Prompt] Can language be violent in its own right?

Yes.

It's the way he uses language [in Ladybird, Ladybird*] – it's almost as if he's saying, 'Right, in a minute you know what's going to happen', and he builds up to it by saying she was two hours late – she knows what's going to happen.*

It wasn't as realistic as the first one.

[Prompt] If he'd just been screaming at her in the first one and not used any physical violence, would you still class that as violence?

I wouldn't want the kids to be watching it anyway.

If it was just verbal and she argued back it would be more acceptable than it was, but it would still be degrading because she's absolutely scared stiff.

[Prompt] So if there's fear there it makes it violent?

Yes. Not as much as physical violence, but if it creates fear then it's violence.

These comments support the argument that the swearing in *Ladybird, Ladybird*, especially the use of 'cunt', was violence. It instilled fear. It degraded the woman being shouted at, and the verbal assault became akin to physical assault, by delivering hurt in the form of fear. It threatened the imminence of real physical hurt.

There is no doubt that these men considered the violent scene in *Ladybird, Ladybird* to be very violent indeed. It was described as disgusting. As for the mothers, the scene drew its power for these men, in part at least, from the very mundaneness of the setting. It was held to be 'almost fly on the wall', and someone said, 'You could imagine that being real life'. This was the result not just of the acting, but of 'everything in the house – the curtains, the everyday things'. If anything, these men were more bothered by the scene than were their female counterparts, but the emotions triggered were of a slightly different order, and, in contrast to the women, there was little evidence to suggest that the experience of parenthood increased the sense of violence of the film.

Outrage & disturbance

They were upset by the image of the children looking on as their mother was being attacked by their father, but, unlike the women, they did not consider that it made the sequence any more violent. For example, having edited out the shots of the children watching, one man said:

> *The violence is still the same, but you're not seeing the petrified look on the kids' faces.*

In other words, taking the children out may have helped reduce the impact of the scene in an emotional sense, but it did nothing to lessen the overall violence. In fact – and this happened in other groups – part of the discomfort stemmed from the fact that these men did not think that children of that age should even be on the set watching actors create the scene or have to listen to such abuse, albeit acted. As with other groups, we did explain that such scenes were shot to protect children, shot separately from the main action and pulled together at the editing stage.

While both the mothers and the fathers in these two groups were disturbed by *Ladybird, Ladybird*, the disturbance caused to the women was, if not greater than the men's, at least of a different order in terms of emotional impact. And we believe this was so because the women's experience of parenthood made the violence stronger. The women were disturbed as women and mothers, but the men were disturbed only as men. They were made to feel uncomfortable by the scene, so uncomfortable that some of them did not consider it appropriate that such violence should be screened:

> *It shouldn't be filmed for video, television or anything.*
>
> *We know it goes on but so does paedophilia. Are we going to film that as well? It's unacceptable.*

It seemed that, to these men, wife-battering was the unacceptable side of men's behaviour towards women, and that to witness such behaviour made them feel on the one hand uncomfortable, and on the other hand angry that such behaviour was common:

> *That's an everyday occurrence in some households.*

> *You don't think it could be you doing it but subconsciously I think you feel a bit ashamed because it's a bloke doing it to a woman.*

> *I know a woman that it's been happening to but until you see something like that you don't realise what she's going through. It's clicked something for me.*

The response of this group to the domestic violence of *Ladybird, Ladybird* was the most 'outraged' of any of our sample. Even though we cannot be sure of what prompted their strong response, one thing we can say with certainty is that fatherhood did not affect their definition of the scene as violent, whereas motherhood did for the women. These men were no different from the men in other groups in deciding what made the scene violent, and nor did they consider the scene to be more violent than did other men: they simply reacted to it more strongly.

12

Violence as entertainment — women

We included subscribers to cable and satellite film channels in the sample because, of all genres, films are the most likely to have violent content. Did these viewers define violence differently from others? They did not, and what they said tells us little that is new about how violence is defined. All that subscribing to a film channel means is that they enjoyed films, and, as it turned out, enjoyed violence in films.

The group of women aged 25 to 34 added nothing new to the discussion of *Ladybird, Ladybird,* for example, but it did give a clue as to how they viewed television. Its primary purpose was to entertain.

My other half went to bed when I watched that.

I don't think my husband would watch that and yet he quite likes violent films.

These women agreed that *Ladybird, Ladybird* would not hold their husbands' attention because, as one woman pointed out, the violence in *Ladybird, Ladybird* was 'not entertainment'. We responded by asking: 'Can violence be entertaining?'

I think it can, yes.

I like Mafia type films — Goodfellas *is one of my favourites.*

Why is that kind of violence enjoyable?

Because its something I wouldn't associate with. You can associate more with people like that [the woman in Ladybird, Ladybird*] than with the Mafia guys in New York.*

[Prompt] Did the violence in Ladybird, Ladybird *seem more violent to you than the violence in* Goodfellas?

Yes.

That's more real life, raw violence.

Again, if I saw something like they had in Goodfellas *I'd run a mile but because it's on screen it's meant to be entertainment. The story is meant to be entertaining and the violence is part of it. I found it very entertaining. There are very few films where I have come away and felt shocked, whereas something like that [*Ladybird, Ladybird*] which is a type of documentary is a lot more true to life. Although if I lived in* America *I might say* Goodfellas *was true to life because I'd seen that happening to someone down the road.*

Don't you think that they're all gangsters in Goodfellas *anyway — they're not doing it to little old ladies or to children, they're doing it to their own.*

[Prompt] So what you are saying is that if it's close to home and you get involved, that makes the violence stronger?

Yes. If they're innocent victims it's going to have a greater effect.

[Prompt] Would you edit Ladybird, Ladybird?

No. Like I said, it's all or nothing. There is no point editing one punch or one swear word.

The swearing — he used the 'C-word' a lot — it's not a commonly used word is it?

I don't think I've ever heard it used on the screen.

[Prompt] Can you have verbal violence?

Yes.

It's abuse, but I wouldn't think it's violent.

It depends how it makes her feel — if it makes her feel under threat by using that language, then I think it is.

I personally say that violence is physical.

If I was in the street and someone used that language on me I would feel that it was quite violent, even if there was no physical side because you expect it to be followed up by violence.

I'm not saying I wouldn't feel threatened.

Violence as entertainment

For these women violence can be entertaining, but only 'harmless' violence. Harmless violence is not the same as the playful violence of *Thief Takers*, but more like the violence of *Deep Cover*. It is harmless in the sense that it poses no threat to the viewer. It is drawn from a different world from the one the viewer inhabits. So the violence in *Ladybird, Ladybird* was considered less acceptable than the violence in *Deep Cover*, even though the images of pain, blood and a savage beating in *Deep Cover* are far more graphic than the images in *Ladybird, Ladybird*.

This group of satellite and cable viewers enjoyed their films, and although not 'buffs', they were aficionados. They made distinctions between types of violence, and talked knowledgeably of genres and what one might reasonably expect from a type of film. For example, one woman in talking of the violence in *Deep Cover* said:

> *It didn't particularly bother me. In a film like that you expect to see scenes like that. I wouldn't have expected anything less.*

Not surprisingly, she wanted to make no edits. The woman who included *Goodfellas* among her favourite films said, 'The story is meant to be entertaining and the violence is part of it'.

Familiar with violent films, this group classified the violence in such films under styles of production. In discussing the violence of *Thief Takers* one participant said:

> *I'd say it was feature film violence, big screen violence.*

Another person, commenting on *Deep Cover* compared with *Ladybird, Ladybird*, observed:

> *In that* Ladybird, Ladybird *whatever you see, hear, imagine, or whatever, that's pretty violent full stop. Whereas something like that [Deep Cover] is a bit of Hollywood violence – you know that guy has been hit around the head with a baseball bat so you know what's happening.*
>
> *[Prompt] What do you mean by that?*
>
> *The usual big feature film violence – just like the clip of* Thief Takers *before we played about with it. Let's get as much impact as we can.*

The process of bracketing violence by production styles is not the same as defining what makes something violent, but it enabled this group to know what to expect, and what to accept as entertaining.

They reacted to the swearing in *Ladybird, Ladybird* in differing ways. Those who felt language could be a threat of violence, considered it violent. Those who did not feel threatened by language thought only physical force could be violent. One of the women said that if a person felt violence was going to happen, that was sufficient to define something as violent. Another woman said that if such language (as in *Ladybird, Ladybird*) was directed at her in the street she would 'expect it to be followed up by violence'. Once again we see that if an act implies violence, it is considered violent. It creates fear, and to all intents and purpose fear is a physical happening. To swear in the manner of the man in *Ladybird, Ladybird* is to administer a blow.

Knowing what to expect

We showed this group both the clips of the dead and injured following the bombing in Bosnia. Given that swearing for some of this group was defined as violence, we were especially interested in their response to scenes of injury, since neither of the scenes included any actual violence. The first clip was the Sarajevo bombing footage transmitted by Croatian Television. They found the pictures shocking, but were they violent?

> *I wouldn't say it's violence because there are no actual violent acts going on. It's the after-effects which makes it more shocking, and the fact that it's news — you know that it's happening now. It might not be on your doorstep, but it's going on. But it's not violence.*
>
> *[Prompt] So it's got to be action shots to be violence?*
>
> *It's got to be a slap! I'm not saying that I would like to have seen what's gone on before that — you don't have to have seen it to know. That is a news report of the aftermath of violence.*

We then showed the more gruesome scenes of injury from Reuters, reporting the consequences of the mortar bomb explosion that ripped into young people sitting outside a cafe. The same woman said:

Again it's aftermath.

This time, however, someone who had been silent before disagreed and said:

I thought it was violent – I thought the other one was as well. It's war and war is violent. I know it's the aftermath but it is the aftermath of violent acts.

[Prompt] So you would roll it all in together?

Yes.

For her, then, 'violence' did not need to include the moment of injury. Her view coincides with the earlier argument that the aftermath of violence is seen as violent if it immediately follows the violent act. Yet for her the aftermath of this violence was itself violent because it was war – 'It's war and war is violent'. She was alone in this, however, and for every one else the act of violence itself had to be witnessed.

13

Violence as entertainment – men

In the opening discussion with this group of men aged 25 to 34, one of them revealed why he subscribed to a movie channel:

I like to see the movies as they should be seen, uncut . . . I don't like them cut. I can decide for myself what I want to watch, and also they broadcast the proper sound so it's just like being in the cinema.

[Prompt] Do you think the stuff on cable and satellite is more violent than the terrestrial channels?

Yes, you're still getting Top Gun *on BBC1.*

As if to disagree with the implied comment that films on terrestrial channels were 'tame', another man interjected:

Channel 5 shows some good ones – they had Natural Born Killer *on last week.*

[Prompt] Yes, that was cut though wasn't it?

I watched that at the cinema – it was good.

[Prompt] What was good about it?

It's quite violent – what's his name? – he's a really good actor, he's an excellent actor. It's filmed from different angles.

[Prompt] Do you enjoy watching violent films?

Yes. If you get a write-up about something and they say there's a lot of violence and sex in it you find most people will watch it out of interest.

These men had firm ideas about the type of film they liked:

You can tell by the actors – Steven Seagal is not going to do a lovey dovey movie is he?

[Prompt] Has anybody seen any real life violence?

This was taken as a foolish question:

Every Saturday night in the taxi queue.

[Prompt] Bad violence?

Just fisticuffs really. Well, I've see a couple of bleeding teeth and stuff like that.

I think most people have been involved in something like that.

[Prompt] Have you seen glassings in pubs and things?

Yes, people are always smashing glasses aren't they?

Women are always the cause. I'd say 75 per cent is men fighting over women.

[Prompt] People always think York is a nice place, but there's bouncers on most pubs in York.

We've got bouncers on Mothercare down here.

It was agreed, however, that Bristol was not as rough as other places:

It's not bad in comparison to somewhere like Manchester or Birmingham, but where you have a big city where a lot of young people are out drinking at night there's always going to be trouble.

Hating real violence, enjoying fictional violence

Although familiar with street violence, these men were not 'hard' like our London group of designated 'hard' men. They were older than the London group and of a different social mix, but their age and the type of entertainment associated with that age group did take them to venues and areas of the city where violence could be expected. They enjoyed violent films, but they knew the difference between screen violence and real life violence, both visually and morally, and they did not enjoy or approve of the use of physical force in real life. Referring to screen violence, one man said:

You know it's false. That's the difference between that and a snuff movie. I've never seen a snuff movie, but you know in your mind whether it's make up or not.

I almost feel embarrassed to say it but I really love violent films. I liked ID and Pulp Fiction *and* Reservoir Dogs, *but when I see violence in the street I really hate it, it makes me feel sick. I just don't like it at all. It makes me angry that people can be like that.*

I have to get into a violent film – it's no good just sitting there watching it, you've got to get into it to enjoy it.

[Prompt] When you say that you like violent films, what is the attraction?

I wouldn't say it's the violence itself, it's the whole attitude of the film – it's the whole ethos of the film all the way through, not just the violent parts.

As we have seen from the various groups of respondents, the enjoyment of violence is not evenly distributed. Although quite a few of our female respondents enjoyed scenes of violence, absolute enjoyment was more a male preserve.

Appreciation of a genre

It would be wrong to isolate violence as the single appealing feature of a film, and to ignore the film as a whole. It is not just bloodshed or savagery which is appreciated, but more the type of film characterised by such scenes. A key to this lies in the remark: 'Steven Seagal is not going to do a lovey dovey movie is he?' The assumption is that if Steven Seagal is in a film one knows it will not be sentimental. If we juxtapose this with – 'I wouldn't say it's the violence itself, it's the whole attitude of the film' – we have our explanation of why some people, especially men, are fond of violent films, or, more accurately, films which contain violence.

Films with a high degree of violence are 'hard' and not 'soft'. The themes dealt with and the emotions displayed are not sentimental, but represent a 'realistic' view of the world. Although not universally so, this is very much a male view of the world.

Did these men – who liked to view violent films uncut – define violence differently from the other groups? The simple answer is, no. But the man who said, 'I feel embarrassed to say it but I really love violent films', went on to name violent films to illustrate his taste. Along with *Reservoir Dogs*, he included *Pulp Fiction*. Yet no-one in any of the other groups rated *Pulp Fiction* as violent, and nor did anyone in this group when it was discussed, because the comedy surrounding the violence prevented it from being defined as violent.

Another of the respondents in this group, after viewing *Thief Takers*, said that he had not enjoyed the scene, and added:

> *There is a bit too much of that sort of thing on now isn't there?*

We thought this strange, given earlier indications that violent drama was to his taste. It turned out, however, that it was not violence he was objecting to, but the type of violence:

> *It's a bit unbelievable.*

As one of the women cable subscribers replied when asked whether there was there too much violence on television:

> *It depends what you call violence – I'd say no.*

This group found most fictional violence acceptable, and might therefore be expected to look for a greater level of violence than normally seen on television.

14

A guide to the prinicples in practice

A t the beginning of the report we gave a general definition of violence: *Screen violence is any act that is seen or unequivocally signalled which would be considered an act of violence in real life, because the violence was considered unjustified either in the degree or nature of the force used, or that the injured party was undeserving of the violence. The degree of violence is defined by how realistic the violence is considered to be, and made even stronger if the violence inflicted is considered unfair.*

The substantive chapters then illustrated the principal elements which lead to this a definition. As we promised in the opening section of the report, we will now present a formula for how violent material might be rated. And finally, to help demonstrate how violence is defined empirically, and how material might be coded in line with those definitions, we have taken our three grades of violence – violence with a little v, with a big V, and a massive V – and allocated three programmes shown in the course of the video editing groups to each of the three grades of violence, with reasons. For example, we allocated *Thief Takers* to small v because the Primary Definers of violence were not obviously present, and then other characteristics, allocated later in the model or scheme, failed to increase the level of violence.

*A Model of the Process of Defining Violence (Morrison &
Svennevig)*

Key elements:

1   Identify purpose/genre of content.

2   Identify structural components which determine whether there
is the potential to be v or V (or hyper V): PRIMARY
DEFINERS.

3   Identify structural components which determine whether it
actually is v or V and how much loading there is SECONDARY
DEFINERS.

Three types of violence: Judged by evidence of Intent, Genre and Approach

PLAYFUL	DEPICTED	AUTHENTIC
• Not related to direct personal experience/expectations	• Detailed portrayal of violent acts	• Known personal world either physically or psychologically
• Surreal or unreal	• Choreography to be taken as real	• Detailed portrayal of violent acts
• Not meant to be taken seriously	• Not related to direct personal experience	• Choreographed to be unmistakably real
• Choreographed not to be taken as real	• Happy or just deserts rather than sad or unjust	• Direct link to personal experience
• Stereotyped rather than in depth		• Unpredictable twists, endings

PRIMARY DEFINERS: Defines Type of Violence

UNFAIRNESS:
A moral judgement

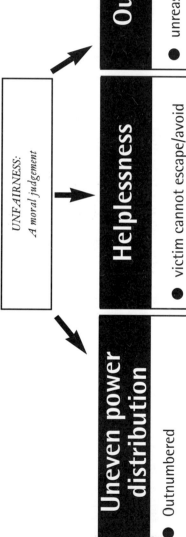

Uneven power distribution

- Outnumbered
- Outgunned
- physically weaker
- psychologically weaker

Helplessness

- victim cannot escape/avoid
- victim physically incapacitated
- victim psychologically incapacitated
- victim too weak to defend

Out of Order

- unreasonable level of behaviour
- undeserved level of action
- status of participants
- disregard for others
- over-punishment

REALISM: *Structure of Portrayals*

Aggressor characteristics	Distance	Detail	Pace	Mood
• ferocity • sadism, cruelty	• close quarter • removed • familiarity	• amount of exposure • close-up • amount of injury seen • amount of attack seen • type of wound/effect • sounds of injury • sounds of victims • duration	• slow motion • replay • multiple views • suspense	• atmosphere eg lighting, place • sounds /reactions of bystanders etc • swearing/ threats • facial expressions • music • atmosphere eg lighting, place

PLAYFUL

ENJOYMENT OF CONTENT

- positive
- neutral
- negative

APPRECIATION OF STORY

- positive
- neutral
- negative

DEPICTED

ENJOYMENT OF CONTENT

- positive
- negative

APPRECIATION OF STORY

- positive
- negative

AUTHENTIC

ENJOYMENT OF CONTENT

- not applicable

APPRECIATION OF STORY

- positive
- negative

WORKED EXAMPLES: Primary Definers

little v Thief Takers

- Primary definers not obviously present

big V Deep Cover

- Primary definers strong
- physical incapacity
- unreasonable behaviour

hyper V Ladybird, Ladybird

- Primary definers very strong
- uneven power
- physical incapacity
- helplessness
- unreasonable behaviour
- disregard for others

little v Thief Takers	big V Deep Cover	hyper V Ladybird, Ladybird
AGGRESSOR • none	**AGGRESSOR** • ferocity • sadism	**AGGRESSOR** • ferocity • cruelty
DISTANCE • removed	**DISTANCE** • close quarter • unfamiliar	**DISTANCE** • close quarter • familiar
DETAIL • low blood and injury • close-up violence	**DETAIL** • pain • cruelty • close-up blood and injuries • close-up violence • slow motion • sound of injuries • sounds of victim • duration	**DETAIL** • pain • cruelty • intimidation • close-up injuries • close-up violence • slow motion • sound of injuries • duration
PACE • suspense • mainly slow motion • multiple views	**PACE** • real time • slow motion	**PACE** • real time
MOOD • music	**MOOD** • bystander reactions • lighting • facial expressions	**MOOD** • bystander reactions • swearing • facial expressions

Appendix 1

Recruitment information for video editing groups

Location & Date	Group no.	Sex	Age	Marital Status	Children	Other criteria
Leeds 26/11/97	1	F	18-24	Single	None	'hard'
Leeds 26/11/97	2	M	18-24	Single	None	'soft'
Manchester 27/11/97	3	M	25-45	no restrictions	Oldest child 12-16	social grade C2D
Manchester 27/11/97	4	F	25-40	no restrictions	no restrictions	fear of violent crime
Edinburgh 28/11/97	5	M	60+	no restrictions	no restrictions	must be retired C2Ds
Edinburgh 28/11/97	6	F	25-50	no restrictions	Oldest child 5-11	social grade BC1
London 1/12/97	7	M	n/a	Policemen	n/a	n/a
London 2/12/97	8	F	25-34	no restrictions	no restrictions	cable/sat subscribers – must have film channels
London 2/12/97	9	M	18-24	Single	None	'hard'
Bristol 3/12/97	10	F	60+	no restrictions	no restrictions	must be retired BC1s
Bristol 3/12/97	11	M	25-34	no restrictions	no restrictions	cable/sat subscribers – must have film channels
Birmingham 4/12/97	12	F	18-24	Single	None	'soft'

Appendix 2

A guide to material used

In total 20 sequences were available on the computer to show to the respondents in the edit groups. Each was of a sufficient duration to enable viewers to get a feel for the nature of the programme and each was long enough to allow the possibility of editing. It was never intended to show all 20 clips to every group, nor that every clip shown would be edited. Interestingly, much of the material had been seen already by the group members and was clearly remembered. Indeed, some material was mentioned spontaneously in discussion before we showed it.

Categories

(a) Feature films made for cinema release and subsequently shown on television. This category included scenes from:

(i) Three Hollywood films:
Deep Cover
Pulp Fiction
Schindler's List

(ii) Two British realist films:
Ladybird, Ladybird
The Krays

(b) British made for television fiction:
The police series *Thief Takers*
The Channel 4 soap opera *Brookside*

(c) Actuality footage:
While the research focused primarily on fictional depictions of violence, actuality material was included by way of comparison.

This consisted of:

(i) News footage from ITN, the BBC, Croatian Television (HRT) and *Sky News*

(ii) Untransmitted news agency pictures of a an extremely graphic nature

(iii) Documentary and current affairs material:

Panorama (BBC 1)

The Provos (BBC 2)

(d) Television comedy:

Bottom (BBC 2)

(e) Cartoon violence

Tom and Jerry

(f) Highly stylised children's programming

Power Rangers

Some material, *Pulp Fiction, Brookside, Culloden, Power Rangers* had a 'history' in as much as they had been the occasion of media debate or audience complaint.

In addition to the transmitted material, we had several instances of unedited material which had not been transmitted on British television. These included:

(i) The cinema version of *Deep Cover* to compare with the edited version transmitted by Carlton on ITV.

(ii) Croatian Television (HRT) coverage of the Sarajevo market place bombing which was more horrendous than any shown in British television even though it was edited from the same rushes. This was compared to the *Sky News* version of the same story.

Several distinct kinds of violence were selected:

(a) Criminal violence:

Thief Takers (gun play)

Deep Cover (attack with a pool cue)

The Krays (a sword is pushed through a man's hand at the end of a beating)

(b) Domestic violence:

Brookside (husband attacking wife)

Ladybird, Ladybird (husband attacking wife with great violence and bad language)

(c) Stylised violence:

Thief Takers (slow motion and exaggerated special effects)

Power Rangers

(d) Realist violence:

The Krays

Brookside

Ladybird, Ladybird

(e) The aftermath of the most horrendous violent acts:

news agency material from Sarajevo and Tuzla

(f) Comic treatment of violence:

Pulp Fiction

Bottom

Tom and Jerry

There were deliberately a number of variables within each extract.

Brief description of the scenes used

Thief Takers: A group of gangsters in a restaurant are being watched by armed police. A rival group of Russian gangsters armed with machine pistols enter and confront the indigenous criminals. The Russian leader head butts his rival. The police enter and a spectacular shoot-out occurs. Filmed in slow motion with a loud sound track, this action takes place in a shower of breaking glass and at one point depicts blood spurting from the back of a gangster as he is machine gunned.

Deep Cover: A criminal who has spoken to the police is attacked with a pool cue in front of associates. Six graphic blows to the head and body are depicted, four of them in close up, and blood is seen spurting from his face.

Deep Cover (edited): The Carlton Television version of this scene cuts the blows to three, removing the spurting blood and concentrating on the reactions of the witnesses rather than on the blows themselves.

Culloden: A chaotic battlefield scene including graphic details of face and head wounds, followed by a second scene showing an attack by armed soldiers on defenceless women and children.

Ladybird, Ladybird: A violent attack by a man on his domestic partner in front of small children. He hits her with his fist, kicks her and uses a beer can. Violent language is used throughout including the 'c' word.

Brookside: A situation similar to the above but no blows are actually seen, children are present and the language is subdued.

The Provos: This recently transmitted documentary series used archive news footage from the 1970s showing an actual bomb explosion in Northern Ireland. An injured woman and screaming child are shown in relative close up.

Croatian Television News (HRT): This reporting of the Sarajevo market place bombing includes a headless body being dragged from the scene. Respondents were warned of the graphic nature of this material.

Sky News: This report of the same story was assembled from the same news agency package as the HRT package but which uses less graphic detail. The headless body was not used by Sky.

A *Reuters* feed from Tuzla in Bosnia showing the aftermath of a mortar bomb attack on a café. Bodies are loaded into a van, including one in which the victims head appears about to fall off. Respondents were warned of the graphic nature of this material.

Channel 4 News (ITN): A feature story on bear baiting in rural Pakistan which included close up shots of bears who have had teeth forcibly removed. Tethered bears are seen being attacked by dogs.

Sky News: A set of rushes covering the story of an Italian tourist who stole a teddy bear from outside Kensington Palace after the death of the Princess of Wales. As he is interviewed outside court, he is punched in the head by a drunken man.

The transmitted (and shorter) version of the same story was also shown.

Pulp Fiction: The scene in which the John Travolta character accidentally shoots a man sitting in the back seat of the car in which he is travelling. Blood is seen splattered on the back window of the car and on the faces of the driver and front seat passenger. The victim is not seen. A second scene in which a hypodermic syringe is rammed into a woman's chest was also shown to some groups.

Panorama: A woman in Rwanda describes how she was forced to commit atrocities which she relates in detail.

Schindler's List: A group of women concentration camp inmates are told to undress, their hair is cut and they are lead into a large shower room. Tension builds until the water is turned on to the relief of all.

Bottom: A man's head is smashed on a bar several times until he spits out a large number of teeth. The process is repeated on a second man.

Tom and Jerry: Violence is done to both figures including being burnt by being held in a spoon over a lit candle.

Power Rangers: A young woman transforms herself into a 'power ranger' and engages in close physical combat with a gang of attackers who she despatches. Confronted by their leader, an armoured creature she fights on. Stylised martial arts kicking and punching seems to have no effect on the recipient of the blows.

Which groups saw which clips

Clip	Group											
	1	2	3	4	5	6	7	8	9	10	11	12
Thief Takers	V	V	V	V		F	V	3E	V	E	V	V
Deep Cover	V	E	2E	E	E		E	2E	2E	V	E	V
Deep Cover (edited)		V	V	V	V	2E		V	V	V	V	V
The Krays	V		E								V	
Culloden				V	V	V		V		V	V	
Ladybird, Ladybird	V	E	V	E	E	4E	E	2E	V	V	V	V
Brookside	V	V	V	V	V	V		V	V			V
The Provos	V			V	V	E		V	V	E	V	V
Sarajevo (HRT)	V	E	V	V	V	V	V	V	V	V	V	V
Sarajevo (Sky)		V		V								
Tuzla (Reuters)	V	V	V	V	V		V		V		V	V
Bear baiting	V	E	V				E				V	V
Teddy Bear (rushes)	V	V	V	V	V	V	V	V	V		V	V
Teddy Bear	V	V	V	V	V	V	V	V	V		V	V
Pulp Fiction	v	V	E	V	V	V	V	V	V	V	E	
Panorama		V					V					
Schindler's List		V					V					
Bottom		V			V	V				V		
Tom and Jerry												
Power Rangers												

V   Viewed clip
E   Edited clip
2E, 3E   Edited clip 2, 3 &c times

Appendix 3

Biographies

David E Morrison graduated in Sociology from the University of Hull, and completed his doctoral studies at the University of Leicester's Centre for Mass Communications Research. He is currently the Research Director of the Institute of Communications Studies at the University of Leeds.

Brent MacGregor is Professor of Visual Communication at Edinburgh College of Art, Heriot-Watt University. A former BBC Producer, he has worked in higher education researching and teaching moving image, culture and practice since 1986. He was an original member of the Institute of Communications Studies, University of Leeds.

Michael Svennevig graduated in Psychology from the University of Newcastle. He has held research posts at both the BBC and the ITC, before becoming Head of Media at Research International. He is currently Research Fellow and Research Director of the Centre for Future Communications, part of the Institute of Communications Studies at the University of Leeds.

Julie Firmstone graduated from the Institute of Communications at the University of Leeds with a B.A. (Hons) in Communications Studies. At the time of the research she was research administrator of the Centre for Future Communications.